# GREECE

## A journey through History and Civilization

EDITIONS
TOUBI'S®
ΕΚΔΟΣΕΙΣ

*Shortcut from the Opening
Ceremony of Athens 2004 Olympic
Games, that took place at the
Olympic Stadium.*

© Copyright      MICHAEL TOUBIS PUBLICATIONS S.A.
                 Nisiza Karela, Koropi, Attiki
                 Telephone: +30 210 6029974,
                 Fax: +30 210 6646856
                 Web Site: http://www.toubis.gr

ISBN: 960-540-039-1

# The face of Greece

This book is mainly concerned with the visual splendour of Greece-its contrasting landscapes, the treasures of its past, the people, the incredible brightness of its light, the sculptured coasts and blue seas, and the present scene-everything that combines to make this land uniquely attractive. Not the most beautiful, not the most famous, not the most important-just the one people enjoy most. How does one account for the magic of this land?

It is true that Greece typifies the contrasts, geology, climate, even paradoxes inherent in the Mediterranean region. But contrasts between town and country, barrenness and fertility, and between man dominating nature and nature dominating man, are more marked in Greece than anywhere else.

Although it is a geological prolongation of the Balkan peninsula, it is a distinct world that fills the mind with unforgettable impressions. The light is almost unnaturally clear and luminous, spilling over mountains and flashing off the sea on to the coasts and islands. The air is clean and fresh and scented with the aroma of countless wild flowers. More tangible is the aura of history that enfolds you: the superb sophistication of Minoan Crete, prehistoric Mycenae and megalithic Tiryns, classical Athens, Byzantine Mystra and medieval Rhodes. Partly it is the timeless background-ancient ruins and crumbling stone walls, Bronze Age volcanoes, and the tang of the sea. Dotting a historical span of almost 4000 years is Greece's incredible tradition of arts and crafts, ranging from prehistoric pottery of ingenius shapes and vivid Minoan frescoes to the incomparable sculptures of the Golden Age and Byzantiums jewel-studded treasures.

## The Contrasts

Greece is always more than one expects. And with good reason. Around every corner it seems there lurks some hidden treasure: splendid ruins that indicate past glory and long human occupance, a shop full of appealing folkcraft, a beach sited bungalow resort, a stretch of sapphire sea, or a wayside taverna inviting you to lose all sense of time over a glass of wine. This combination of antiquity and modernity keeps the visitor hovering between reality and fantasy until he reconciles the long history of Greece with its living present.

Then again, Greece consists of several bits of diverse geography. Soaring mountains are separated by deep valleys, lakes and seas, its ternal imprint. There are countless peninsulas and bays and indentations. And, of course, innumerable islands. It is really a land of islands, one after the other, no two alike.

The waters that almost surround the 132,000 square miles of Greece are blue, pure and clear. They moderate its temperatures in all seasons, and the constant sunshine gives a diamong sparkle to everything. To think of Greece is to think of its climate, which is typically Mediterranean and just as warm and delightful in April and October as it is in July and August.

## The People

There are some 11 million Greeks: cheerful, hospitable, funloving, unpredictable perhaps, but full of contagious enthusiasm. One hardly ever comes across a bored or surly Greek.

From the beginning, indeed, from the time when Greece was first inhabited, some 7000 years ago, her hardy people have been intent on proving that they are a special breed, fully capable of guiding their own destiny they still are. And they still do. Their boundaries may have altered, and they have undergone the most diverse experiences in the course of history, but this has moulded them into a single nation embracing countless generations. The spirit that made this craggy land what it was 25 centuries ago, a very small corner of the earth that exercised an influence out of all proportion to its size, still persists. Greece is once again a living entity, responding to the call of the centuries, yet remaining herself through time.

## The Present Scene

Along with the scenery, the history, the beautiful islands, brilliant sunshine and blue seas, Greece also has to offer modern facilities in all parts of the country. That is why it is now fast becoming one of the favourite holiday countries in Europe and the Middle East. Almost all the hotels are new and equipped with every up-to-date amennity. Even a third class hotel with a bath is the rule rather than the exception. Travel by boat, train, airplane or car ferry is easy and comfortable. Reasonably cheap too. The beaches are crowd free, and there are well-placed camping sites for the go-it alone traveller. Yachts and cruise ships are catered for by some 85 supply stations and marinas, on islands and coasts.

The ideal way to see Greece and to gain some insight into the true spirit of the Greeks is by car or bus combined with ship or airplane. The magic of Greece works on you the moment you set foot in the country, and by combining ample leisure time with well planned sightseeing you will find that Greece has few equals for the wealth and variety of impressions it leaves in the mind. And these will remain cherished memories long after the holiday itself is over.

*1. The famous Corinth chapiter.*　　　　　　　　　　　　*2. View of the town and the castle of Patmos.*

# Historical background

1

$\mathcal{T}$he dawn of Europe's history, when the kingdoms and empires of the Oriental civilizations rose and fell, begins with the arrival of the Greeks. The first slow stages of the climb from primitive culture to the heights of civilization began in the Aegean area during the Bronze Age (2800-1100 B.C.). It was an age of trade and communication between nations, peaceful on the whole, but with interludes of savage warfare. The Aegean area was the key position for all trade during the 2nd and the 3rd milleniums B.C., between peoples coming from the North, Asia Minor and North Africa. The whole of the Aegean Civilization was based on sea power and commerce. The ancient world brought its trade to the islands and coastal regions of the Aegean, and the wealth of the inhabitants increased accordingly. Crete was in constant trade communication with the rest of the Aegean, where independent little civilizations arose, of which the most notable is the Cycladic. The Cyclades group was too small to support a large population, but their mineral and metalic wealth, added to their geographical position, gave the islands unusual importance in the early Bronze Age.

Depending then on the region where the Aegean Civilization had developed, and on the particular features of its remains, they are now called Minoan, after Grete's legendary King Minos ; Cycladic, for the group of islands which lie roughly in the middle of the Aegean Sea; Mycenaean, on the Greek mainland where Mycenae stood-the strongest city of the time according to Homer. Lastly, there was the Trojan Civilization in the regions of Troy, to the North-west of Asia Minor. The Bronze Age ended everywhere some time during 1100 to 1000 B.C., when the last wave of invaders from the North, the Dorians, came down to Greece. Their advent dealt the final blow to the Mycenaean Civilization. The Dorians were a warlike tribe, but they brought with them the Iron Age and a civilization which exercised an immense cultural influence. Meanwhile, at about 1000 B.C., the Pelasgians and Ionians left the Greek mainland, under pressure from the Dorian invasion of Peloponissos. They crossed the sea and settled in the North-Aegean islands and along the coast of Asia Minor. The Greek colonists had a genius for settling in the right spot, and a good eye for places with commercial possibilities. Great cities grew on the Asian coast and on the islands, and by the 7th and 6th centuries B.C. they were centres of brilliant civilizations. They were in contact with the great civilizations of the East, and they brought to this Eastern culture the Greek vigour and freedom. In size they far exceeded most of the cities of old Greece, and their civilization was richer and finer, except perhaps for that of early Corinth. The galaxy of rich and powerful cities included Clazomenae, Halicarnassus, Colophon, Smyrna, Phocaea, Samos, Ephesus and above all Miletus. They were the cradles of science and philosophy, the first triumphant flowering of the individual city-state. Thought was free, and the human spirit found itself. Men had found their freedom and so had leisure to reflect, to reason about the purpose of life, the aims and ideals which give vitality to civilization. But the tragedy of these independent and flourishing states was that they were too individualistic. They even lacked the power of combination against a foe, and so they were doomed to fall under the domination first of the Lydians and then of the Persians.

But in their short centuries of freedom they had time to do a great work: they helped to open up the Mediterranean and the Black Sea to Greek civilization. Greek colonies sprung up from the western Mediterranean to the shores of the Black Sea, and the seeds that were to transform the whole outlook of western man had firmly taken root by the 6th century B.C. The end of this period saw the emergence of two rival powers-Sparta and Athens.

Starting with Homer and his ballads of the Iliad and the Odyssey, Greece burst forth into a new era of rapid progress which led to what is now known as the Classical Age (500-323 B.C.). It is this period which has left the most important monuments and relics, and which set ideas and principles which hold goo to this day.

This «Golden Age» was at the same time the most turbulent. There was internal strife as well as invasions. Thus in 490 B.C. Greece suffered the first Persian invasion but thanks to the efficiency and capabilities of the various Greek armies, particularly of Athens, the Persian hordes were repulsed at Marathon, where the Greeks won a great victory.

The period from 480 B.C. to 431 B.C. was dominated by the brilliant statesman Pericles who initiated the great building schemes which included the Parthenon and the Propylea on the Athenian Acropolis. Externally the empire of Athens flourished as reluctant allies were forced to obedience. Internally the radical democracy was based on a popular assembly open to all and on a panel of "generals" elected annually by vote. Athens was at the time filled with architectural gems, and was also the centre of culture, welcoming all that was new in science, philosophy and art. For more than half a century it enjoyed political supremacy, but its significance in western history arises from its many-sided activity of thought, art and life.

*1. Gold sealing ring, that was found at the Mycenaean cemetery of Aidonia, near Nemea, and dates from the 15th century BC.*
2. Pericles speaking at the Pnyx Hill, *a painting destroyed in the 1941-44 bombings of Athens.*

2

The Peloponnesian War (431-404 B.C.), which heralded the decline of Athens, came as an outcome of Spartan fear of the power of Athens. The great plague in 430 B.C. and a fatal disagreement over strategy after the death of Pericles in 426 B.C., finally brought Athens to her knees, and under the oppressive overlordship of Sparta, the trivial quarrels of the Greeks almost achieved what the might of Persia had failed to accomplish, so that the history of the West was in fact, staked on the issues of Marathon, Salamis and Plataea.

Weakened by the long war, the 4th century B.C. saw all Greece threatened by the new power of Macedonia. Many eminent Athenians preached alliance, but the stronger voice of the greatest Athenian orator, Demosthenes, led Athens to resist Macedonia. This led to the disastrous battle of Chaeronia in 338 B.C. The fortunes of Athens and several other city-states were now those of Macedonia. Their days as important independent cities were ended, having failed to achieve unity as a single nation, even though there was a common language, worship and way of life from the Ionian Sea to the shores of Asia Minor and from Crete to Macedonia.

History had to wait the advent of Philip of Macedonia to take advantage of this lack of unity and subdue all the Greek cities south of his own kingdom at Pella. A single nation then emerged in an elementary form under his rule and, shortly after, under the rule of his son Alexander the Great. The period from the 4th to the 2nd century B.C. is known as the Hellenistic Age. When Alexander died in 323 B.C. he was ruler of a large Empire and the nation had become known as Hellas. But quarrels among his heirs and various independence movements weakened the Empire, until finally it broke up. Greece then passed under Roman rule. The quality of art declined favour of quantity and size, but the Romans were also great builders of public works. It was then that Greece acquired her first roads, acquaducts, bridges and public baths. In their art, however, they were monumental extroverts, tending towards the massive and ostentatious, embellished with triumphal arches, graphic reliefs and frescoes, and almost always commemorating a Roman victory. The outlook of the Greeks of the pure Classical period was order and proportion. The sculptors sought the ultimate perfection in subject and execution, and seldom fell short of it. Mere size did not impress them. They had indeed some mighty monuments, but in them too, it was in form rather than in bulk that they sought perfection. Even during the Roman domination the Greek city-states retained their pre-eminence in philosophical studies, the fine arts and science, and while Nero hauled the monuments of Athens to Rome, the violet-crowned city of Pericles remained the "University" of the Roman Empire.

The Roman period (146 B.C. to 138 A.D.) also saw the advent of Christianity in Greece. St. Paul preached on Mars Hill in Athens and in other parts of the country, and a generation later St. John wrote the Revelation on the island of Patmos.

When the Roman Empire was divided into Eastern and Western Empires, Greece remained part of the Byzantine Empire which was so much influence by Greek thought and culture that Greek became the language of official affairs, replacing Latin. The Byzantine Age (395 A.D. to 1453 A.D.) lasted 1000 years. This also developed its own art, literature and customes, all of which were strongly influenced by the strong ties between State and Church. Church architecture developed the well-known Byzantine type of cross-transcept with round dome, and the Basilica type of church with the higher centreaisle and one or two aisles on either side lined by pillars and columns. Mosaics and frescoes in churches developed to a high standard during this age which came to an end when the Ottoman Empire conquered Byzantium in 1453. With the fall of Constantinople, capital of the Byzantine Empire, in A.D. 1453, the Turks ruled most of Greece and scholars, writers and thinkers fled westward with their precious manuscripts and books. This was the factor that gave rise to the great Renaissance period which, in turn, influenced western culture.

Earlier in its history, the Byzantine Empire had to condend with Catalan, Frankish and Venetian armies who plundered Greece under pretext of crusades or other purposes.

Greece remained under the Ottoman rule until 1821, when separate revolts merged to become the Greek War of Independence (1821-1834).

Modern Greece begins with the overthrow of the Turkish yoke. The country was re-congnised as an independent State by the Great Powers (Britain, France and Russia) in 1830, and the first monarchy was set up under King Otto of Bavaria. For several decades afterwards the Greek nation strove to bring under its wings areas which had always been inhabited by Greeks. The most recent acquisition of such territory was the Dodecanese Group of islands. They were united with Greece at the Second World War.

This small country with a long history, a country which has always foughtforthe great ideal of freedom, is today set on a progressive course and can point to solid endeavour where the development of her national life is concerned.

By reason of its geography, the spirit of the people who compose this country, and its position in the Eastern Mediterranean, Greece has taken on an enduring character which makes each generation of Greeks dependent on their forefathers and pledged to their descendents. Therefore, the State which is unswerable for Greece, is in charge at one and the same time of yesterday's heritage, today's interests, and tomorrow's hopes.

*Mystras: a wall-painting from the Pantanassa ('Queen of the World') convent.*

*"The Fisherman", fresco from the excavations in Acrotiri of Santorini (16th cent. BC, National Archaeological Museum).*

# Greek sculpture and painting

## An outline of ancient greek sculpture and painting

Greek art developed over a period of 600 years and produced a national genius, a pure, classical school which was to inspire sculptors, painters and architects up to the present day, and perhaps for all time.

As early as the 7th century B.C., men and animals and nature became the main subjects of designs that were supremely visual: accurate observation combined with an amazing clarity of design. A deer hammered on a sheet of gold to make a drinking vessel contains in its bulging, simplified planes all the rhythmical vitality one expects from the workshops of today. The Greek artisan was accustomed from an early age to using his eyes to fight and hunt. The naked landscape around him, infused with the magical light of Greece-a light so intense and pure, it throws forms and shapes into sharp relief-imposed its discipline on the mind and eye. When he chipped and shaped and smoothed, every strain and twitch of a horse's head, every gathering of muscle, blossoming flower or gust of wind, expressed simply, with restraint and symetry, the power of the mind's eye. Order and balance asserted themselves in flawless expressive lines. Mere size never impressed the Greek artist. It was in form rather than in bulk that he always sought perfection. This undeniable striving after truth, a searching for form, even beneath the draperies, is evident in all the statuary of the great periods of Greek sculpture.

Historians of artistic development draw a sharp line of division between the arts of the Minoan and Mycenaean cultures and that which followed their abrupt end about 1000 B.C. With the coming of the Dorians, Greece itself relapsed into a state of semi-barbarism for more than two hundred years. Not until the 7th century B.C. did the current of culture return and flow from east to west. Greece experienced then a period of artistic development and great achievement such as has never been equalled in the history of the world.

Beginning with the minor bronzes and pottery of the Geometric period (1000-800 B.C.), so called because of the simple application of geometry to the problems of the human form, Greek art then reached the Archaic phase (800-600 B.C.), when Greek sea-farers brought back with them from Egypt and the East works decorated in styles completely different from those of the geometric art. This period gave us the well-known "kouroi" (statues of young men and women), which point clearly to Egyptian influece: stereotype pose with one foot set before the other, fixed smile, arms joined to the sides, and clenched fists.

The Egyptian figures were of the hardest stones-porphyry and granite, but the Greeks did not have to face this challenge. The fine white marble of the islands could be carved easily with light tools and emery. Gradually, the rigid posture acquired variety in its composition, when the sculptors gave a more realistic treatment to the human form.

It was from these important years that the beginnings of Greek monumental sculpture and architecture stem, and in which we recognise the origins of the Classical art.

With the dawn of the 6th century B.C. the emancipation from the Archaic was well on its way. However, the great period of Greek sculpture begins in the Classical Age (500-400 B.C.), when Greek sculptors sought the ultimate perfection in subject and execution-and seldom fell far short of it.

By the 5th century B.C., the stark majesty of the monumental sculptor gave way to the graceful power of Pheidias and, a little later, to the refinement and delicacy of the gods and goddesses of Praxiteles. Sculptors exerted themselves to get the utmost out of the marble in their hands. They even tortured it to express ideas hardly expressible in stone-and they were amazingly successful. Polycleitus, Myron and Pheidias were the three masters of this period. The famous «Doryphorus» of Polycleitus was one of the earliest statues in which the weight of the body, instead of resting on both feet, is thrown on to one foot, while the other leg is «free standing» with the heel raised from the ground. The result is a wonderfully easy pose. Myron was the first to discard the rigid uprightness of chest and head, and to show the full flexibility of the body in action. His statues of athletes, among them the well-known «Discus Thrower», are notable examples of his art.

Fifth century B.C. sculpture reached its culminating point in Pheidias, who was undoubtedly the leading spirit in the sculptural decoration of the Acropolis, and was responsible for the colossal statue of Athena (40 ft high), by which this group of buildings was once dominated. It is considered likely that the sculptures of the Parthenon, if not actually «Pheidias» work, were made under his direction.

In the 4th century B.C., the sculptor's ideal became modified. Instead of aiming merely at the interpretation of a robust physical life and spiritual serenity, he sought the expression of human emotion and passion. The most well-known sculptors of this school are Scopas, Lysippus and Praxiteles. Scopas, in particular, is famous for the passion he put into marble faces, with deep-set eyes and agonized foreheads. To him has been attributed a head from the temple at Tegea (in the Athens National Museum) and world-masterpieces such as the Niobe group and the Victory of Samothrace are ascribed at least to his influence. The most famous works of Praxiteles are the Venus of Cnidus, at the Vatican in Rome, and the Hermes with the infact Dionysos at the Olympia Museum-works that show less passion and more dreamy tenderness than is seen in the art of Scopas. Lysippus, who is said to have executed a vast number of statues, including many of Alexander the Great, delighted in the rendering of physical vigour, as in the «Apoxyomenus», also in the Vatican.

The ultimate in the representation of human suffering was reached in the group which shows the legendary Laocoon, with his sons, writhing in the coils of the deadly serpents. By this time, Greek art had entered the Hellenistic Age (300-150 B.C.), when Alexander the Great united all the Greeks and their civilization spread beyond the borders of Greece. The change in political conditions caused by the formation of independent states under Alexander's generals is held to have been responsible for a certain decline in the artistic

The "Poseidon of Artemision",
bronze statue representing
Poseidon brandishing the trident
with his raised right hand. It
is an original work of a great
sculptor, possibly of Kalamis. It
was raised from the sea, off the
cape Artemision, in north Euboea
(dated to ca. 460 BC, National
Archaeological Museum).

ideal. But there are works of genius and real beauty belonging to this age. Art could be great and monumental, just as architecture tended to the gigantic and to great feats of engineering. The Mausoleum of Halicarnassus, one of the seven wonders of the world, with its frieze of struggling Greeks and Amazons, crowned by the immense and serene statues of Mausolus and Artemisia in their chariot, belongs to this same age. The little kingdom of Pergamum, in Asia Minor, boasted a great temple and an immense open-air altar of Zeus, surrounded by a crieze of sculpture on a truly colossal scale. Other masterpieces of loveliness include the Victory of Samothrace, the Dying Gaul and the Aphrodite of Melos, all of which vie in beauty, dignity and restraint with the greatest achievements of the age of Pheidias.

At the other end of the scale art became more homely, and sought inspiration in the everyday aspects of life. Sculptors produced thousands of terra-cotta figures richly illustrative of Greek daily life and charmingly free from the classic conventions. From this phase of Greek art, we have such examples as the pleasant little statue of a child struggling to hold a goose, or a boy pulling a thorn from his foot, or an old woman, bent with age but vital in every wrinkle.

A very attractive form of this lighter Greek sculpture is seen in the Tanagra figurines, thousands of which have been found in graves.

It was in the Hellenistic Age, too, that the arts of cutting cameos and striking coins achieved perfection.

## Greek painting

There is no extant Greek painting on which to form a judgement, apart from the Greek vases and the Pompeian wall-paintings executed by Greek artists during the late Hellenistic period. But there is no lack of literary records, and many names of Greeks painters have come down to us.

We know that they used the fresco technique for wall paintings, and tempera for panels, and-in the best period-the encaustic method, painting with dry wax-sticks and burning the colours into the carefully prepared surface. Later came the mosaic work which was to become vulgarized in the decoration of Roman houses-a debasement which led Horace to remark that "conquered Greece led her conqueror captive" in the arts. This has been taken to mean that the Romans were merely copying from the older Greek civilization.

The decorative paintings of Polygnotus and Micon were, it is safe to assume, coloured outline drawings, without modeling, shadow or perspective. According to the records, Agatharchus, at the end of th fifth century B.C., was one of the first artists to study the problem of perspective. Then came Apollodorus, a pioneer in light and shade, and those reputed masters of realism, Zeuxis, Parrhasius, and Apelles.

Although we have no means of comparing a single example of Greek painting with medieval or modern work in that medium, we have at any rate the evidence of the red and black figure pottery to guide us in our estimate of the painters' progress in general. This ware, produced in great quantities from the 6th to the 4th centuries B.C. and distributed through the Mediterranean countries, represents in many cases the loveliest combination of ceramic design and pictirial embellishment ever devised.

# Greek folk art

Traditional Greek Popular art, examples of which a visitor may come across in each of his steps, has to offer a unique sense of form and colour. From his dress to the decoration of his home and items of daily use, the Greek can be distinguished for his good taste.The artisan expresses himself with all kinds of materials, with copper, marble, wood, wools, silk, silver, iron and clay.

These traditional popular arts are not museum items. In every corner of Greek earth the artisan and embroiderer continue, by traditional means, to create their works. Flokatis, blankets, rugs dresses, beads, jewelry, shoulder bags, decorative items, pottery, in an inexhaustible variety of colour and design are offered to this country's visitors, not only as souvenirs of their trip, but as items which serve their basic needs as well. Textiles from Mykonos, flokatis from Macedonia and Thessalia, embroidery from Lefkada and Rhodes, alabaster from Crete, jewelry from Ioannina, ceramic pottery from Sifnos and Skopelos.

Every corner of the country presents its own objects, worked by local craftsmen who keep alive the old traditions, since our popular art is a pure expression of the Greek soul, that wove, embroidered: carved gold and silver, formed clay with fire, and created, carrying down its message from generation to generation.

Genuine examples of the textile art, such as shoulder bags, chest aprons, capes, cushions and carpets are in great demand. Greek jewelry is famous for its craftmanship. The craftsmen work the silver, copper and gold with love and obtain their inspirations from archaic and Byzantine periods from Greek nature and also from popular dress designs.

From the depths of past centuries, ceramic art comes alive in our time. In Crete, Rhodes, Sifnos, Skopelos and Lesbos, self-taught craftsmen as well as known artists create small ornamental objects which bear the seal of popular imagination and the unrepeatable valve of handcraft.

There is a permanent pottery exhibition, in Marousi, near Athens, where one can see and buy ceramics from all over Greece.

# Greek folk dances

One of the most powerful means which help men all over the world to know each other, to understand and love each other is art, the language of which is understandable to all the people alike.

Dance is an art as old as man himself which, still today covers a great part of all peoples' life. Folk dance in particular expresses the most contrasting and the multifold sides of life throughout the .world, that is subjects and feelings which stirred the peoples deeply at the evolution of their historical existance. Folk dances are full of genlteness, of moving heroism, pure lyrism and spontaneous humour. Folk dance is not just a series of sensational pictures, but it also depicts the pure creation of the popular genious. When the greek youth pours out into the stage with the traditional dances of Greece, one can discern, hidden behind the poetical picture of the dance, the peculiarities of our national civilization, the charm of the greek nature with the praised mountains, the picruresque islands, the beautiful plain and the bright blue sky.

Each greek region has its own folk dances with their individual folklore. Every folk dance in its total, together with the accompaning music and costumes, discloses the characteristics of the life, the customs and very often the character of the people.

# INDEX

Didimoticho

Drama    Xanthi    Komotini    **9**

Serres    Filippi
Kilkis              Kavala    Alexandroupoli

Prespes    Edessa
Florina          Pella    **8**
        Veria    Thessaloniki    Thasos
Kastoria          Polygiros
    Kozani    Vergina              Karyes    Samothraki
        Dion    Katerini
**6**    Grevena                Mountathos

Zagorochoria    Meteora    Larissa    Limnos
Metsovo
Ioannina    Dodoni    Trikala    **5**
Igoumenitsa              Karditsa    Volos    Pelion    Lesvos
Parga    Arta                    Skiathos    Alonissos
Preveza    Karpenisi    Lamia    Olympos    Skopelos    **10**
Lefkada    **3**        Aedipsos    **4**    Skyros
        Amfissa    Thermopyles        Kymi    Chios
**7**    Messolonghi    Delphi    Arachova    Chalkida
                Livadia    Eretria
                                Andros
    Patra    Kalavryta    Pireas    **1**        Samos
efalonia        Korinthos    Athina            Tinos    Ikaria
Zakynthos    **2**    Mykines    Salamina    Aegina    Kea    Syros    Mykonos    Patmos
    Pyrgos    Olympia        Epidavros    Sounio            Leros
        Tripoli    Nafplio    Poros    Kythnos    Serifos    Paros    Naxos    Kalymnos
    Kalamata    Sparti        Hydra        Sifnos        Amorgos    Nirsyro
Methoni    Mystras    Spetses        Serifos            Astypalea
                            Milos    Ios
                Monemvassia    Folegandros        Thira    Anafi
            Kythira            **12**

eros
ymnos    Kos                Chania
    Nisyros                Samaria    Rethymno    Agios    Kassos
alea    Tilos    Rodos    Elafonissi    Gorge        Herakleio    Nikolaos    Vai
                            Knossos    **13**
            Karpathos
**11**

Kassos

| 1 | ATTICA |
| 2 | PELOPONNESE |
| 3 | CENTRAL GREECE | 7 | IONIAN ISLANDS |
| 4 | EUBOEA - SKYROS | 8 | MACEDONIA - THASOS | 11 | DODECANESE |
| 5 | THESSALY - SPORADES | 9 | THRACE | 12 | CYCLADES |
| 6 | EPIRUS | 10 | ISLANDS OF THE NE AEGEAN | 13 | CRETE |

# 1 attica

Attica is the Greek area upon which ancient Athens nurtured philosophy and democracy. In this little corner of the earth the vitality of the Greeks found expression in all creative fields, and their thoughts helped to transform the whole outlook of Western man by the immortal and splendid Attic Civilization.

First Inhabited in the 4th mlllenium B.C. by Pelasgians and later by Ionians, possesses strong links with the historical past and there is hardly a part of the region where evidence of human activity centuries old cannot be found. Place names and historical remains at Marathon, Eleusis, Brauron, Amphiareion, Ramnous, Sounion and Athens itself commemorate an older Greece, which In those long-gone eras exerted an influence out of all proportion to its size.

However, this deservedly popular part of Greece does not live in the past. Along with the scenery, the history and the clear blue sea there are modern tourist facilities to be enjoyed in first class hotels, beach bungalow resorts and sports grounds. Excellent roads bring most of the beauty spots and historical sites of Attica within easy reach from Athens.

Attica's few small plains are intensely cultivated with grapevines, vegetables and fruit trees. And dark olive groves everywhere. Attica is also the most highly industrialised part of Greece and accounts for the bulk of the country's industry.

The rivers Ilissos and Kifissos flow across this beautiful part of Greece. They are not very big but they are historically associated with Attica's distant past.

The Attica coastline has been famous for its beauty from ancient times. Geographically the region forms a triangular peninsula terminating south at the temple-crowned Cape Sounion.

## ATHENS

Greece begins in and revolves around this city, one of the most ancient capitals of the Western world. Cupped in a bowl on the west coast of Attica, with the mountains Aigaleo, Parnitha (Parnes), Pendeli and Hymettus on three sides and the Saronic Gulf on the other, it forms one continuous city with its seaport Piraeus and the suburbs. Together they have a population of about three million. New and ever expanding, the modern part of Athens has largely been built in the past forty years or so. The urban sprawl of high rise buildings reaches green suburbs as far as the surrounding mountains and the western coast ot Attica. In almost every direction there is something to see: sparkling sea, lofty and delicately shaped mountains, the indelible imprints of an ancient past, and all the sophistications of twentieth-century living.

Athens was first inhabited some 6,000 years ago by Pelasgians and later by Ionians,

who found the great rock of the Acropolis, or Upper City as the name implies in Greek, a natural stronghold. As the city grew, it was dedicated and named after the Goddess of Wisdom, Athena.

It enjoyed its first flourishing period in the Mycenaean era (1600-1100 B.C.). At the end of the 6th century B.C. tyranny was overthrown and the democratic form of government which followed led to unprecedented achievements in the history of mankind. In the 5th century B.C. -the "golden age" of Athens-, under the enlightened leadership of Pericles, Athens had its full development in the fields of culture, commerce and military strength.

During the Hellenistic and the Byzantine periods Athens was a secondary city. After the Greek liberation from the Turks in 1834 it was proclaimed capital ot Greece.

## The Acropolis

Everything and everyone in Athens seems to be drawn irresistibly towards the Acropolis, the 156-metre high limestone rock that crowns the city. Clearly visible from any part of Athens, the delicately poised and dazzling white columns of the Parthenon stand out against the blue background of the sky, an immortal symbol of the spirit and genius of man. Archaeological excavations carried out on the slopes and on the flat summit of the Acropolis have disclosed that this great Sacred rock was first inhabited in the Neolithic Ages some 6,000 years ago. First the Pelasgians and later the Ionians came to settle here living in the caves mainly along the northern side. In times of danger they sought refuge on its summit. Its natural springs attracted tribe after tribe to its slopes and with the passing of the centuries the small settlements spread to the neighbouring regions of Pnyx Hill, the Agora and Keramikos. Uninterrupted occupation led to the growth of the city until by the middle of the 6th century B.C. Athens extended as far as the foothills of Lycabettus and Mount Hymettus. The first stone temples were built in the begining of the 6th century B.C., replacing wooden ones. The Parthenon was dedicated to the Goddess Athena. Some of the sculptures from its pediments are housed in the Acropolis Museum. During the Persian wars the Acropolis was sacked (480-479 B.C.). The splendid monuments we see here today date from the great era of reconstruction under Pericles, be-

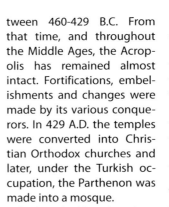

tween 460-429 B.C. From that time, and throughout the Middle Ages, the Acropolis has remained almost intact. Fortifications, embelishments and changes were made by its various conquerors. In 429 A.D. the temples were converted into Christian Orthodox churches and later, under the Turkish occupation, the Parthenon was made into a mosque.

During the Venetian siege of Athens in 1687, some of the buildings were partially destroyed by cannon balls and a fire which raged for two days.

## The Parthenon

The apparent simplicity and design of the Parthenon, a building famous the world over for architectural beauty and harmony, is the temple of the virgin (in Greek "parthena") Athena. It is built of Pendelic marble in the Doric Style on the same site as two previous temples. It took 15 years to build (447-432 B.C.).

## The Temple of Athena Nike

The delicate and graceful structure to the right of the Propylaea (the monumental entrance to the Acropolis) is the small temple of Athena Nike, also known as temple of the "Wingless Victory", built in the 5th century B.C. to commemorate the Greek victories over the Persians. Its frieze depicts scenes from the battles. In this small temple the Athenians paid homage to Athena Nike without wings, so that she might not fly away from Athens.

## The Erechtheio

The Erechtheio is distinguished for the stately magnificence of the Caryatids, the young priestesses who support the temple's roof with their heads. The Erechtheio was a temple dedicated to the mythical hero-king Erechtheus (who was later identified with Poseidon). The Athenians were told that in this place Athena and Poseidon contested for the protection of Athens. Athena won, by producing from the earth an olive tree.

*1. Representation of the Acropolis (Ancient Greece, Mc Rae Books, Srl. Florence, Italy).*
*2. The Parthenon.*
*3. The Temple of Athena Nike, a symbol of Athenians' faith to their state.*
*4. The famous Caryatids, a bold architectural project.*
*5. The Acropolis and the surrounding area, today.*

4

## The Acropolis Museum

The Museum stands in the southeastern corner of the Acropolis and houses priceless archaeological finds kept in chronological order, starting with the Archaic (800-600 B.C.), and going to the Classical (500-400 B.C.), Hellenistic (300 B.C.) and Roman periods. Among other outstanding works of art housed in the

Museum's 9 rooms are sculptures and sculptured reliefs from the pediments, frieze and metopes of the Parthenon, the Erechtheio and the Temple of Athena Nike. Also on display is the unique collection of the «Kore» statues (young girls with the characteristic Archaic smile).

Room II exhibits the famous «Moschophoros», a man bearing a calf on his shoulders. This is an exceptionally fine work, noted for its composition and plasticity of form.

In Room V are pedimental figures of the «Gigantomachia», or Battle of the Giants from the old Temple of Athena, built by the Peisistratids. More works of the so-called «Severe Style» are on display in Room VI, among them a sculptured relief showing a "Contemplating Athena» who seems absorbed in her thoughts as she is resting her head on her spear. The most characteristic of works belonging to the «severe» style are the «Kritias Boy», and the "blond boy", so called because of the yellow colour of the hair.

In Room IV are the majority of the «Kore» statues, among them the «Peplos Kori», so called from the girded Dorian peplos (mantle) she wears over her chiton. The statue is famous both for its facial expression and its original colours.

## Odeum of Herod Atticus

This theatre at the foot of the Acropolis was built in the 2nd century A.D. by Herodus Atticus as a memorial to his wife Pegilla. It is in the typical form of an ancient Roman Theatre with a seating capacity today of 5,000 spectators. The seating was restored in 1950-1961. Originally it was used for musical and drama performances as well as for contests. Today it is the main theatre of the Athens Festival presenting each summer concerts, recitals, musical and drama performances.

## Theatre of Dionysus

A theatre of ancient Greek drama where the plays of the great dramatists (Aeschylus, Sophocles, Euripides, Aristophanes, Menandrus) were first presented. It lies at the foot of the Acropolis, to the south, next to the "Sanctuary of Dionysus".

Originally the theatre had wooden seats which were replaced by seats of stone in 342-326 B.C., much in the form we see today. It could accommodate some 20,000 spectators in 78 rows of seats. The first row consists of 67 marble «thrones», where the high officials sat (priests, leading citizens, notables).

The orchestra, the open semicircle between the stage and the audience, was rebuilt by the Romans. They organized gladiatoral performances as well as mock naval battles in this theatre.

## Athens Museums

The main museums of Athens are the National Archaeological, the Byzantine and the Benaki Museums. There is also the Acropolis Museum, the National and Historical Museum, the Museum of Greek Popular Art, the National Picture Gallery, the Theatrical Museum, the Geological and Paleontological Museum and others.

*1. The three-bodied demon, section of the pediment of the archaic temple.*
*2. The "Contemplating Athena" (460 BC., Archaeological Museum of Acropolis).*
*3. General view of the Theatre of Dionysus.*
*4. The Theatre of Herod Atticus.*

## The National Archaeological Museum

It is one of the most important museums for ancient Greek art internationally. Unique in the world is its Mycenaean collection (gold jewelry, precious stones), the collection of Cycladic art (statuettes and idols), its collection of Archaic art (the famous statues of young men named "Kouroi" and pottery) and the recently discovered superb frescoes and other finds from Thera (Santorini). The rich collection of vases covers the periods from the pre-Geometric era to the 4th century B.C.

The visitor can also find a collection of bronze objects as well as a collection of Egyptian and eastern antiquities.

## The Byzantine Museum

It is housed in what was once a mansion of Florentine architecture, built in 1848. It displays the features of Byzantine art and objects for use in churches, including works of art from Byzantine and post-Byzantine sculpture, paintings, small handicrafts, icons and frescoes. Many of the exhibits come from churches which formerly stood in Athens or its surrounding regions.

## Benaki Museum

This was founded in 1930 by Antony Benaki. It is lodged in a neo-classical building and contains a rich and interesting collection of Ancient Greek and Byzantine art, jewelry, Oriental exhibits, and much Chinese porcelain from the Neolithic Age to the 18th century A.D. Also on display are textiles, embroideries, carpets, weapons from the Greek War of Independence, and jewellery of Coptic, Muslim and Turkish art.

1. *"The Ephebe of Antikithira" (300 BC, National Archeological Museum).*
2. *A group of Afrodite, Panas and Eros (100 BC, National Archeological Museum).*
3. *A votive relief depicting Orphea (4th – 5th century AD, Byzantine Museum).*
4. *Fagum portrait of a young man (middle 3rd century A.D., Benaki Museum).*
5. *The National Archeological Museum.*

## Monuments around Acropolis

To the west of the Acropolis lies the **Areopagus**, the small rocky hill on which the oldest Athenian council met. A lower hill, the **Pnyx**, is where the General Assembly gathered. The highest of the low hills which face the Acropolis is crowned with the monument of **Philopappos** -a marble memorial, dating from the 2nd century A.D.

The Graceful and gigantic columns of the **Temple of Olympian Zeus** stand to the east of the Acropolis. The temple was started under Peisistratos in 530 B.C. but was not completed until Roman times under Hadrian in 129 A.D. **Hadrian's Arch**, which stands near the Temple of Olympian Zeus, was erected in the Roman era to mark the boundary between the "City of Hadrian" and the "City of Theseus", as the inscription reads above the slender columns.

Other sights below the Acropolis include the impressive octagonal tower with its inscriptions and figures of the wind gods. Built in the 1st century B.C. as a hydraulic clock, complete with sundial and weathervane, this monument is commonly known as the **Tower of the Winds**.

The **Monument of Lysicrates** is a small 4th century marble edifice in a square where Lord Byron stayed during his first visit to Athens. This circular choragic monument was erected by the Athenian Lysicrates, winner in a Chorus competition at the Theatre of Dionysus.

*6. The Lysicratis' choregic monument.*
*7. The Hadrian's Gate and the Temple of Olympian Zeus.*

## Plaka

Plaka for the Athenians is the quarter of the gods. Plaka, sited at the foot of the rock of the Acropolis, was from ancient times the centre of Athens. At every step, in every alleywayl, at every turn there is a fresh surpise: churches, ancient remains, neo-classical buildings, Frankish houses, with the life of present-day Athens of Plaka, weaving in an out of all this. Here the visitor is charmed by local colour and the picturesque. Plaka is full of tavernas, boites, night clubs, cafeterias, squares, trees, columns, churches, tourists, barrelorgans. And you encounter the shops of Plaka at every step - its innumerable shops. For your souvenirs there are handicrafts carpets, furs, goldware, silverware - this is the artists' quarter.

## Monastiraki

At the end of Pandrosou Street you will meet the Monastiraki Square and the train station connecting Piraeus and Kifissia. The Monastiraki area begins at Monastiraki Square, continues to St. Philippa Square, then Ermou Street and Thessio, Pireos Avenue and tangles in the alleyways. In its center, Abyssinia's Square with its old antique shops dated from the beggining of the 20th century, houses the Sunday bazaar. The shopping trade continues at Ermou Street. In the middle of this shopping mall stands the Kapnikarea church, with the chapel of Agia Varvara. The church today belongs to the University. At the right side of Ermou street lies the Athens Cathedral, next to the Byzantine church of Agios Eleftherios.

## Lycabettus Hill

On the summit of the cone-shaped hill stands the chapel of St. George. The climb to the top of Lycabettus can be made on foot or by cable-car. Once there the view is rewarding. Refreshments and meals are served at the hilltop snack bar and restaurant.

Some of the 19th century buildings in central Athens were designed by Bavarian architects during the reign of King Othon. Of these structures, along Stadiou Street, the best known are the **Greek Academy**, the **University Building** and the **National Library.** All three are in the neo-classical style.

**Syntagma Square** is the heart of modern Athens. Around it are luxurious hotels, offices and rows of open-air cafes. The **House of Parliament** (once the Royal Palace) and the **Monument of the Unknown Soldier** are situated above the square.

**Athens Stadium** was completely rebuilt for the first modern Olympic Games in 1896. It stands on the site of the ancient stadium built in 330 B.C. Its track measures 2-4 metres by 33.50 metres. It can accomodate some 60,000 people.

The **Temple of Hephaestos**, better known - by mistake - as "Thessio", overlooks the ancient Agora. It is the best preserved of all Greek temples.

*1.The Temple of Aeolus (Tower of the Winds). 2. View of the Ancient Agora. 3. General view of Kerameikos, the cemetery of ancient Athens. 4. View of Monastiraki. 5. The Athens' Academy. 6. The House of the Parliament, at Syntagma Square; in the background the Lycabettus Hill. 7.The Lycabettus Theater. 8. The Panathenaic Stadium.*

# PIRAEUS

This principal port of Greece, and one of the largest in the Mediterranean, is a city in its own right. It has a population of nearly one million and is only 10 km from Athens. Its strategic importance was established during the Classical era, about 450 B.C., when Themistocles built the famous Long Walls which linked both cities. Large sections of these walls can be seen today, as well as ruins of other ancient buildings, including two ancient theatres. The ancient harbours of Zea and Munichia are today called **Passalimani** and **Mikrolimano**, or **Tourkolimano**. Zea is one of the largest marinas in the Mediterranean, while Mikrolimano is well-known for its fish restaurants along the waterfront, next to colourful boats and small yachts anchored in the small harbour. It can be reached along the beautiful corniche road which skirts the coast from **Zea** to **Kastella** and **New Phaleron**.

Apart from being one of the busiest ports in the Eastern Mediterranean, Piraeus and its surrounding districts also constitute the centre around which most of the country's industries are concentrated. All kinds of industrial plants, factories, metal foundries, warehouses and dockyards are spaced out in all directions. But the city's centre is something of a surprise. It is well laid out and spotlessly clean with several small parks and broad tree-lined avenues. Sea-going passengers, especially those sailing to the Greek islands are well catered for by a number of efficient services available at the various embarkation stages.

*1. The neoclassical building of the Piraeus Municipal Theater.*
*2. The Pireus Port.*

*Right, above: The Stadium of Peace and Friendship, at Neo Faliro.*
*Below: The harbour of Zea (Passalimani).*

Both the **Archaeological** and **Naval Museums** are worth a visit, and one should not miss seeing at least one performance at the "**Veakeio**", the open-air theatre on the top of **Prophitis Elias hill**. From here the panoramic view of the Saronic Gulf and the Apollo coast is truly breath-taking at night.

The nearby towns to Piraeus (**Drapetsona, Keratsini, Perama, Nikaia, Korydallos, Kaminia** and others) have their own atmosphere with factories, little harbours and popular quarters.

1. Votsalakia, the beautiful beach of Kastella.
2. The coastal road at Piraiki.
3. View of Zeas' harbour.
4. Vouliagmeni's area.
5. Lavrio, a city-monument of ancient and current industrial history.
6. Sunset at the temple of Poseidon, Sounio.

## APOLLO COAST
## SOUNION - MESSOGHIA

By far the best way of seeing Attica is to make the round trip, by bus or car, along the Apollo Coast on a fast road with lovely scenery, which hugs the Saronic Gulf, and on reaching **Sounion** continue inland through the Messoghia, or midlands, to return to Athens. The high point of this drive is the 5th century **Temple of Poseidon** crowning the top of the headland at Sounion, with a view looking far out into the Aegean Sea.

The drive back from Sounion to Athens along the inland route takes you through the rolling hills of the Messoghia—the typical Attic countryside. There are two interesting places along the way: **Paeania** and **Pan's Cave** (Cave Koutouki) and **Lavrion** (Laurium) famous in antiquity for its silver mines.

The **Messoghia** is dotted with tiny villages where a good meal and excellent local wine can be enjoyed in the open or inside small tavernas.

# REST OF ATTICA

## Marathon

Beyond Nea Makri lies Marathon, an area of great historical importance. It was the site of the historic Battle of Marathon in 490 BC. In commemoration of this battle, the Athenians erected the burial mound of Tymvos, which is 12 m. high and has a circumference of 185 m. for the Greeks who lost their lives in that battle. There is also an interesting Museum near the site.

## Rafina

Rafina lies to the right of Pikermi (26 km). It is one of the oldest harbors of Attica and serves a large number of the Cycladic islands with a regular schedule of ferry boats.

## Brauron

In the region behind Mt. Imitos known as the Messogia lies the town of Spata and beyond it the beach of Artemis. To the right is Vravrona (ancient Brauron) and the temple of Artemis, one of the most ancient and revered sanctuaries in Attica, dedicated to the protectress of the natural world of crops and vegetation and everything connected with it.

## Amphiareion

This sanctuary near Oropos, north of Athens, was dedicated to Amphiaraos, god of healing. The sanctuary with its Doric temple was a combination of oracle and health spa, as there was also a spring with therapeutic waters on the site. A small theatre, ruins of Roman baths, hostels, the stoa used by patients and a water-clock are all that remain of this important centre of healing.

## Rhamnus

Rhamnus is another important sanctuary of Attica which is dedicated to Themis, goddess of justice, and Nemesis, who punished the presumptuous. The temple dedicated to Nemesis is on the road to Schinias, south of Rhamnus. The temple dates from the 5th century BC; in its sekos were found statues of Artemis, Arsinoe, priestess of Nemesis, and the boy Lysicleides.

## Eleusis

Eleusis, a modern industrial town with a history spanning four millennia, is 22 kilometers west of Athens. It is situated on a plain known as the Thriasian Plain, on the road that goes to the Peloponnese and mainland Greece. In ancient times Eleusis was one of the most important sanctuaries of the goddess Demeter and her daughter Persephone, associated with the changing seasons of the year. It was the site where the Eleusinian mysteries were celebrated. The archaeological site at Eleusis is one of the richest in Greece. In the Museum, visitors can admire important exhibits dating from the archaic, Classical, Hellenistic and Roman eras.

## Megara

After Eleusina the road leads to Korinthos passing by Megarida. At the start of the 1st millennium BC Megarida was conquered by Dorians and joined to a powerful state with Megara for its center. Socratis' student Euclid established the famous "Megara's Philosophical School" (440-380 BC). In 146 BC, Rome conquered Megara. At historical times, this area was an independent state with Megara for its capital.

## Dafni Monastery

Only 11 km from Athens along the Athens-Corinth highway, this beautiful Byzantine Monastery, dated from the 11th century, lies in a tree-shaded grove. In additional to its architecture the church of the Monastery is decorated with some of the most brilliant examples of mosaic art of the Byzantine period. Near the Monastery is a tourist pavilion, the site where the Athens Wine Festival is being held in summers.

1. The tumulus (grave mound) of Marathon. Inlaid photo: "The Ephebe of Marathon" (325 BC, National Archeological Museum).
2. Rafina, the second biggest port of Attica.
3. Statue depicting the goddess Artemis of Brauron.
4. The healer Amphiaraos. Detail from a dedicative votive relief (5th cent. BC).
5. The Ramnus archaeological site.
6. View of the Dafni Monastery.
7. View of the archaeological site of Eleusina.

## THE SARONIC ISLES

**Salamina** (ancient Salamis) lies nearest to the coast of Attica and can be reached by motor launch in about 20 minutes from Piraeus. The narrow strait which separates the island from the mainland marks the site of the celebrated Battle of Salamis (480 B.C.), when the combined Greek fleets defeated the Persians at sea. The island has many beaches, but motor boats can be hired for a leisurely cruise round Salamina, stopping here and there for a swim and a meal of shell-fish, for which this largest of the Saronic islands is famous.

**Aegina** is scenically attractive, with lush vineyards, pistachio groves and pinewoods. Historically, it has been important island from ancient times. Its town for a few months was the first capital of modern Greece following the Greek Revolution of 1821.

1. The temple of Aphaea, Aegina.
2. The harbour of Aegina.
3. Poros, with Galatas opposite.

**Poros** is green and wooded and lies very close to the Peloponnese side, with acre upon acre of lemon trees whose aroma fills the air for miles around. Of sightseeing interest on Poros itself are the Monastery of Panaghia and the ruins of Poseidon's Temple, besides the several lovely beaches and shaded woodlands.

**Hydra** hardly needs any Introduction. Long and rocky, it is a favourate with artists and the younger people. The island is distinctive for its architecture, ruggedness, and incomparable colours.

**Spetses** is the last of the islands in the Saronic Gulf. Small and thickly wooded, it also boasts several fine beaches and rocky coves. It is a popular summer resort, teeming with social activity in the summer months.

1. The harbour of Hydra.
2. Spetses; A view of the town with its picturesque carriages.

# 2 peloponnese

This large peninsula technically forms an island in southern Greece and resembles a huge mulberry leaf. For this reason it was called in the Middle Ages Moreas (from the Greek word for mulberry). Its ancient name was Peloponnese or Peloponnissos (the island of Pelops, the mythical King of Phrygeia, who later ruled over Ilia and Arcadia). From antiquity, there have been efforts to cut the Isthmus that connected Attica to the Peloponnese. This was eventually effected in the 19th century A.D. when the canal was completed.

This broad peninsula covers an area of 21,439 square kilometres and has a population of about 1,500,000. Its greater part is a region of valleys separated by towering mountain ranges rising to 2,407 metres at Taygetos. Hills are intersected by fast flowing rivers with historic associations: Alphios, Pinios and Evrotas. The plains of Ilia, Messinia and Argolis are among the most fertile in Greece. The region's 7 provinces are: **Achaia, Argolis, Arkadia, Ilia, Corinthia, Lakonia** and **Messinia**.

There is evidence of human activity in the Peloponnese going back to 100,000 B.C. Archaeological remains from the Old Stone Age and the New Stone Age have been discovered at Ilia, Nemea, Lerna and elsewhere. The Peloponnese reached its most flourishing period during the Mykenaean Age (1600-1100 B.C.), with the growth of such cities as Mycenae, Tiryns, Pilos and Sparta all of which enjoyed a high level of civilisation.

From prehistoric times, the Olympic Games were held in Olympia for peaceful competition between athletes from cities from all over Greece and her colonies. During the Classical period, the rivalry between Athens and Sparta led to the Peloponnesian War and the start of Ancient Greece's decline. With the coming of the Macedonians, the Peloponnese lost its independence and Alexander the Great was recognised as the leader of a "united" Greece. But the region's decline continued despite a short interval of prosperity under the Achaian Confederation and the efforts towards further improvement by the kings of Sparta, Agis and Kleomenis. The final blow came in 146 B.C., when the armies of the Achaian Confederation were defeated by the Roman general Mummius. The Peloponnese together with the rest of Greece became a Roman province. From then onwards the Peloponnese suffered a series of invasions by barbarians.

The Byzantines, following the Romans, made the Peloponnese one of their provinces.

The Frankish rule that followed in 1204 under Godfrey de Villehardouin saw the division of the Peloponnese into 12 fiefdoms governed by Barons from France, Flanders and Burgundy, which accounts for the region's several Medieval Frankish fortesses. The three largest castles were at Monemvassia, Maina and Mistras. This last one became later a Byzantine town and saw many years of glory and splendour. From Mistras the last Emperor of the Byzantine Empire Constantine Paleologos went to Constantinople in 1453 and he died fighting against the Turks of Mohammed the Second, who then occupied Byzantium and Greece.

For almost five centuries, the Peloponnese and other parts of Greece were under the Turkish occupation. In 1821 the Greek War of Independence actually begun in the Peloponese. Following the Greek liberation, Nafplion was for a few years (until 1843) the capital of Greece.

## Loutraki

Just beyond the Isthmus bridges and facing modern Corinth across the gulf rise the steep slopes of the Gerania range, sheltering in its foothills the well-known **Spa of Loutraki**. Its mineral waters have made Loutraki a popular tourist and health resort. Bordered by sea and mountain, this green strip of coast boasts a number of excellent hotels and restaurants, beaches and bungalow complexes. A few kilometres away to the west lies **Perachora** and the vast **lagoon of Vouliagmeni**, which is ideal for all kinds of sea sports. Beyond the lagoon are the ruins of the **Temple of Hera**, by the side of an almost intact ancient harbour.

*1. Funerary gold mask from Mycenae, known as "Schliemann's Agamemnon", found Grave Circle A at Mycenae (16th century BC, National Archaeological Museum). Above: the Corinth canal. p.40-41: An cultural event at the ancient theater of Epidaurus.*

1

## NEW CORINTH

Modern Corinth is a busy provincial town of some 20,000 inhabitants. Built in 1928 after the old town was destroyed by an earthquake, Corinth is a plesant, quiet town and an important crossroads linking the Greek mainland with the Peloponnese. Good hotels and restaurants, a lively esplanade and recreational facilities make it an excellent base for trips to the nearby resorts and historical sites.

Coming over the Athens-Patra highway, it's worth seeing the beautiful **Xylokastro**, the agricultural and commercial center of **Kiato** (near the **ancient Sikiona** and **Stimphalia Lake**) and others.

2

## ANCIENT CORINTH

The ruins of this once splendid city lie high up on a hill above the modern town, overlooking both the Corinth and the Saronicos Gulfs. In fact, ancient Corinth owed its power and wealth to this advantageous position between two large harbours, **Lechaion** in the Gulf of Corinth and **Kechreae** on the Saronic Gulf.

Corinth existed in prehistoric times, and it reached the peak of its economic and cultural progress under the rule of Kypselus (7th century B.C.) and his son Periandrus.

The principal sights include the **Temple of Apollo** (6th century B.C.), the columns of which are monolithic, a rare architectural feature in ancient times. The **fountain of Pirene**, the **market place**, **theatre** and **odeum**, several Roman buildings, and the tribune from where St Paul delivered his sermons to the Corinthians in 51 A.D. are only some of this famous city's archaeological remains bearing witness to its ancient prosperity and power.

3

4

1. The small port of Kiato.
2. View of beach of Loutraki.
3. The Heraion of Vouliagmeni, Perachora.
4. The town and the beach of Xylokastro.
5. The harbor of Corinth.
6. The Temple of Apollo and the Acrocorinth.

# NAFPLIO - Mycenae Argos - Tiryns Epidavros

The bare hill with the remains of Mycenae, the mighty citadel of Agamemnon, rises only 4 km off the main road which leads from Corinth to Argos, at the 41st Kilometre. **Mycenae** was a fortified royal residence, surrounded by huge Cyclopean walls. According to archaeological evidence it seems to have been inhabited since 3000 B.C.

The people lived in small open townships in the plain below the two hills. Mycenae

flourished in the 14th century B.C. Entrance to its Acropolis is through the famous Lions Gate, which symbolises the power of the kings of Mycenae - "a city rich in gold" according to Homer. Beyond the Lions Gate is the stairway leading to the Palace. At the top of the hill can be seen the floors of the Palace. To the right of the entrance are the six shaft graves which comprisesthe Royal cemetery. Within the walls of the Palace are also several houses, store rooms and cisterns. Outside the walls are the beehive tombs, the largest of which is the so-called "Treasury of Atreus". Most of the remarkable and priceless gold and ivory finds from Mycenae are exhibited in the National Archaeological Museum in Athens.

About 6 kms from Mycenae is situated the town of **Argos**. It was - together with Thebes - the most powerful city-state in Ancient Greece before the rise of Corinth. Argos has a few ancient remains and a Museum with exhibits of great interest. It is today known as the commercial and agricultural center of Argolis.

The ruins of prehistoric **Tiryns** are situated at a distance of 8 kms on the road from Argos to Nafplion. It has massive Cyclopean walls encircling the palace, a secret stairway, underground cisterns, tunnels and chambers.

From Tiryns a straight road leads to **Nafplion**, flanked on either side by vast orange and lemon groves which fill the air with their fragrance. Nafplion is really two places in one — a modern seaside resort, and the old town which once served as a Frankish-Venetian bulwark with its fortress dominating the area from the summit of Palamidi. Nafplion, capital of Modern Greece before Athens, has an original charm which makes it a very popular town throughout the year. In summer it teems with tourists strolling along the picturesque narrow streets or sitting at cafés on the seafront. The tiny fortress in the middle of the bay is called **Bourdzi**.

**Epidavros** (Epidaurus) lies in an idyllic landscape, at a distance of 30 kms from Nafplion.

The 6th century B.C. Sanctuary of Asklepios, God of medicine, was a healing centre for pilgrims from all parts of Greece. Prescriptions of medical cures are recorded on inscriptions found in the sanctuary and can now be seen in the small museum. The ancient Theatre of Epidavros is a marvel of harmony and acoustics. It was built in the 4th century B.C. by Polycleitus the Younger and is the best preserved ancient theatre in Greece. It holds about 14,000 spectators.

The Epidavria Festival of today is a revival of the ancient festival which took place every years in honour of Asklepios, with musical and theatrical performances.

1. The Lion's Gate in Mycenae.
2. The Bourdzi fertress, in the bay of Nafplio.
3. Mycenean art: detail of a fresco from Tiryns (13th century BC).
4. Panoramic view of Nafplio with the Bourdzi.
5. Tolo is a modern seaside resort for sunbathing, swimming and sea sports.
6. Panoramic view of the ancient Epidaurus' archaeological site.

## TRIPOLIS - SPARTA
## Mistras - Yithion

Beyond Argos the first town the visitor to southern Peloponnese comes to is Tripolis, the principal township of the province of Arcadia. Tripolis is itself a summer resort popular with those who want to escape from the heat. Other nearby resorts include **Vytina** on **Mount Menalon**, **Leonidi** and **Astros** along the eastern coast of the Peloponnese.

As we journey south from Tripolis, Mount Taygetos and Mount Parnon loom in the distance. This is now Laconia and the next town on the itinerary is **Sparta**, with its rich historical associations. The town was founded by the Dorians in the 9th century B.C. and in the following two centuries it developed into the most powerful military city in Greece, thanks to the cold, austere, yet efficient laws, perfected by the law-giver Lycurgus. The great Peloponnesian War (431-404 B.C.) was, in effect, a conflict between two rival political ideals - of cultured Athens and military Sparta. And though victory went to the austere state of Lycurgus, Sparta too finally fell into decline in 371 B.C. Modern Sparta is a thriving industrial and agricultural centre with broad streets and parks, hotels with modern amenities, restaurants and shops. Nearby Mistras has made Sparta a lively tourist centre. The surviving remains in Sparta date from the Roman and Byzantine periods and are in no way indicative of the former city-state's power and influence.

**Mistras** (6 km from Sparta) was once a glittering fortress of the Byzantine Empire, with palaces, houses, monasteries and churches founded in the 13th century during the Frankish occupation of the Peloponnese. Mistras is now a vast museum of architecture, sculpture and decorative art, conveying to the visitor a vivid image of a splendid and glorious era.

**Yithion** was in ancient times Sparta's port and naval base. According to legend, it is the site from which Paris and Helen of Troy fled to Egypt, following the most famous abduction of all time. Today this pleasant little harbour is the gateway to the area of the Mani and the **Caves of Diros**. It is also an ideal base for excursions to Monemvasia, the second important Byzantine fortress-town in the Peloponnese.

*1. The area of Astros as seen from ts Venetian castle.*
*2. View of Leonidio.*

*Opposite page: Above:*
*The Malliaropouleion Municipal Theater of Tripolis.*
*The central road of Sparti.*
*Centre: Gytheion and the islet of Kranai, with its lighthouse and tower.*
*The underground river of Glyfada at Diros, described as one of the world's most beautiful cave lakes.*
*Below: The church of Pantanassa, at Mystras.*

## Monemvasia - Mani

**Monemvasia** has often been described as the Gibraltar of Greece. It occupies a huge bare rock which rises sheer and grim out of the sea on the east coast of the south promontory of the Peloponnese. It owes its name to the single passageway by which it can be reached. The medieval town has only a few inhabitants today but there are some 500 people living nearby in the modern settlement of Yefira.

Monemvasia retains to this day much of its medieval character and atmosphere - a living piece of history.

The rock of Monemvasia (= 'single entrance', 'single passage') and the hew town on the facing shore stubbornly defying time. Franks, Byzantines, Venetians and Turks have passed through here, leaving behind them traces of their presence. Within its walls, in the so called "Lower Town", there are several interesting old houses along cobbled pathways and many Byzantine churches with original frescoes and icons. Very interesting is also the medieval Acropolis, a fortress within a fortress, with its 14th century **Church of Aghia Sofia** and a ruined palace.

**Mani**, in the southern Peloponnese, is the only part of Greece which never let an enemy set foot on its soil. Its inhabitants are as austere as the landscape around them and devoted to tradition. The high "towers" are now deserted.

**Areopolis**, the chief center of the Mani, has an interesting old church (Taxiarchai -Archangels).

1. The church of Agia Sofia guarding the view over infinity.
2. Vatheia or Poligyros, a traditional maniot village.
3. The rock of Monemvasia (=single entrance, single passage) and the modern town lying at the opposite shore.
4. Alley in Monemvasia, where you can visit the post-Byzantine Church of Christ Helkomenos (Led to the Passion).

## KALAMATA - Pilos
## Methoni - Koroni

Travelling eastwards along the coastal road, we come to Messinia, a province whose capital is **Kalamata**, a thriving commercial town with some 50,000 inhabitants. The road southwest of Kalamata leads to **Pilos** (51 km), a charming seaside town, known also as Navarino. It is the site of the famous naval battle during the Greek War of Independence, when the combined fleets of Russia, England and France destroyed Turkish-Egyptian fleet.

The small island **Sfakteria** across from Pilos seems like an elongated natural breakwater against the Ionian Sea.

To the south of Pilos are situated the two interesting towns with medieval castles, **Methoni** and **Koroni**, known once as the "Two eyes of Venice" because of their strategic position.

North of Pilos and near to the picturesque village Chora on a hill is situated the **Palace of Nestor**, the wise old king who accompanied the Achaians in their campaign against Troy. The famous Mycenaean Palace was destroyed by fire in 1200 B.C. and the clay tablets found in the ruins established the fact that the Mycenaeans spoken an archaic form of Greek. The most impressive remains are the throne room and the monumental entrance. The small museum at Chora has frescoes and "Linear B" tablets found in the Palace as well as other interesting remains.

*5. The attractive town of Pilos, with a history of only 150 years.*
*6. Panoramic view of the beach of Kalamata.*
*7. The medieval castle of Methoni.*
*8. The town and the castle of Koroni*

## PYRGOS - Olympia

**Pyrgos** (319 kms from Athens, 96 kms from Patras, 153 kms from Tripolis) is a colorful agricultural and trading town, the capital of the Province of Eleia.

From Pirgos the road forks eastwards through the fertile valley of Elis, one of the ancient city-states of the Peloponnese. In the middle of this valley, where the rivers Alphios and Kladeos flow, lies **Olympia**. The Olympic Games were held here in honour of the Olympian Zeus every four years from prehistoric times. Between 776 B.C. (the first written date and the beginning of the ancient history of Greece) and 393 A.D. the Greek calendar was based on the Games. The Oympiads included not only athletic contests,but also reciting of verse, reading debates on philosophical and other topics and from 67 A.D. poetic, musical and dramatic competitions. The modern Olympic Games were revived in 1896 in Athens. Even today the Olympic Flame is lit every four years in the ancient sanctuary and is transported from Greece to the stadium of that year's Games.

In the museum one can see the superb statue of Herrpes by Praxiteles. Famous was also the gold and ivory statue of Olympian Zeus created by Phidias.

## Katakolo

Kataklolo is a beautiful and peaceful town lying on the west section of the Prefecture of Elis, in a distance of almost 13 km from Pyrgos. It is a coastal settlement, standing at the north side of the Kyparissiakos Gulf. Beside the bay and its cape the visitor can enjoy beautiful and sandy beaches.

*1. View of Katakolo.*
*2. The restored columns of Palaestra, at the archaeological site of ancient Olympia.*

Above: The Hermes of Praxiteles (4th century BC, Archaeological Museum of Olympia).

## PATRAS
## Aigio - Diakofton
## Mega Spileo
## Kalavryta - Aghia Lavra

**Patras** is the third most important harbour in Greece, lying on the northeastern coast of the Peloponnese. It has some 160,000 inhabitants and is a busy industrial and commercial centre as well as a port, with ferry-boats connecting with Italy.

A pleasant walk can be made as far as the Upper Town or Psila Alonia, for a view over the city and its environs. Also worth a visit are the Achaia Clauss Co. distilleries outside the city. On the top of the hill above Patras rises a Venetian castle built on the site of the ancient Acropolis. The view from it extends as far as Zakynthos and Cephalonia, two of the Ionian Islands. To the southwest of the castle is the Roman Odeum discovered in 1889. Its brick seats faced with marble are almost intact.

Carnival time in Patras is celebrated early in the Spring each year and draws crowds from all over Greece.

The highway east of Patras is fast, scenic and new. It hugs the sides of green hills for 215 kms (Patras-Corinth-

Athens), while skirting part of the northern coast of the Peloponnese. Those who let scenic beauty take precedence over driving speed will enjoy the route along the secondary old road which runs parallel with the motorway.

**Rion** and **Antirrion**, which link the Peloponnese with central Greece by the largest bridge of Europe, stand face-to-face across a 2 kms stretch of sea, northeast of Patras. The crossing takes just under half an hour and provides easy access to the western mainland of Greece (Nafpaktos, Missolonghi, Arta, Ioannina, Igoumenitsa).

After Patras the next big town along the way to Athens is **Aigio**, a commercial town with a busy harbour, wayside tavernas and beautiful beaches.

**Diakofton**, a picturesque town further along the coast (going to Athens), is the starting point for the climb to the Monastery of Mega Spileo. The ascent is made by a track-railway which climbs slowly up the maginficent Vouraikos Gorge, on Mount Chelmos.

**Mega Spileo** (Great Cave) is so called because there is a cave behind the church in which an icon of the Holy Virgin was found. Successive fires destroyed the original buildings, the centuries-old library and valuable manuscripts.The Monastery we see today was built after the great fire of 1934. The icon of the Holy Virgin, said to have been painted by St. Luke, remained unscathed through all the disasters the Monastery suffered and can still be seen in the cave where it was found in 342 A.D. The Diakofton-Kalavryta road runs almost parallel to the 22 km track-railway.

**Kalavryta** is a large mountain village, very picturesque and cool in summer. It is a popular resort with good hotels, tavernas and restaurants. Another 45 minutes drive along an asphalt road will bring you to the 10th century historical **Monastery of Aghia Lavra**. It was here that Archbishop Germanos on 25th March 1821 gave his blessing to the start of the Greek War of Independence. There is a hostelry on the Monastery premises as well as a very interesting collection of manuscripts and other relics.

1. The church of Agios Andreas, the patron of Patras.
2. The harbor of Aigion.
3. The harbor of Patras, the so-called "Western gate of Greece".
4. The Rion – Antirrion Bridge.
5. Station of "odontotos" train in Zachlorou.
6. The Megalo Spilaio Monastery, one of the best known in Greece.
7. Aerial photo of the monastery of Ayia Lavra.

This part of mainland Greece is one of the largest in the country, extending from the Aegean Sea in the east to the Ionian Sea in the west. In the south it embraces the Saronic and the Corinth Gulfs and reaches northwards as far as Thessaly. Central Greece is mostly a mountainous region dominated by the massive ranges of Giona, Agrafa, Tymphristos, Vardoussia, Parnassus and Iti. Several small and fertile plains and valleys lie between these mountains, their formation determined by the rivers Sperchios, Acheloos, Kifissos, Asopos and Mornos. The largest lakes are Trihonis and Amvrakia in western Greece and Iliki in eastern Greece. The climate is not the same everywhere, for whereas the seabord climate is Mediterranean, the inland and mountain regions experience bitter winters and pleasantly cool summers. The main products in Central Greece are olive oil, wine, cotton, cereals, rice and tobacco. In the mountain regions stock-raising is also well developed. Ore is mined too in many places: lead and zinc at Lavrion, bauxite in the mountains of Parnassus and Giona, and marble from Penteli.

Central Greece was the birthplace of Hellenism in very ancient times. In fact, recorded history begins in what later developed as the most important cities in the ancient world-Athens, Thebes, Delphi.

The region also flourished during the Byzantine period, when cities like Thebes were densely populated, enjoying a thriving industry and trade.

During the Turkish occupation, Central Greece together with the Peloponnese played an important role in the fight for freedom, since the countless Greek insurgents could easily harry the enemy from hideouts on the untrodden mountains of the region.

## Nafpaktos

Only 13 km from Antirrion, Nafpaktos is a bright and open seaside town, better known to many people as Lepanto, the proud name of the great sea battle in 1571, which brought Turkish naval supremacy in the eastern Mediterranean to an end.

The two small castles built by the Venetians on either side of the tiny port, were at one time joined together by a chain which served to shelter ships that sought refuge there. When the Venetians departed in 1700, Nafpaktos became a nest of pirates until its liberation from Turkish rule.

There is a lot to interest the visitor to Nafpaktos. The fairytale castle on the top of the hill is Venetian, but the base on which it stands was built by the Pelasgians in 1400 B.C., with repairs and additions made to the walls by the Mycenaeans, Romans, Byzantines, Venetians and Turks. The view from the battlements is fabulous and so is a stroll around the wooded enclosure.

## MESSOLONGHI
## Aetolikon - Agrinion
## Amphilochia - Vonitsa

This heroic small town in western Greece lies on the shores of a wide and shallow lagoon in the province of Aetolo-Acarnania. In 1826, during the War of Independence, the world was impressed by the heroic exodus of some 2,000 inhabitants who broke through the lines of the vastly superior Turkish and Egyptian forces. Few managed to get through, and in memory of those who perished in that heroic attempt, **Messolonghi** celebrates each year the Great Exodus. The town is also famous for its romantic associations with Lord Byron and other philhellenes who died here.

**Aetolikon** (9 kms from Messolonghi on the Agrinion road) is a picturesque seaside town reminiscent of a small Venice with its lagoon.

The most important centre of the Greek tobacco industry is **Agrinion** (34 km from Messolonghi).

From the charming town of **Amphilochia** (40 km from Agrinion), skirting the Amvrakikos Gulf, one reaches the idyllic small town of **Vonitsa** and its Frankish castle.

*1. Silver coin of the Delphic Amphictyony.*
*2, 3. View of Nafpaktos, with its two small castles at its port.*
*4. The cental square of Agrinio.*
*5. View of Amphilochia.*
*6. The Exodus of Messolonghi, a painting by Theodoros Valyrakis (1814 – 1878, National Gallery – Alexandros Soutzos Museum).*

## Thebes

**Thebes**, the once powerful city-state that fell along with Athens in the battle of Chaeronia in the 4th century B.C., has little to show of its past glory and wealth. The remains of a Mycenaean palace can be seen in Pindar Street, and near the Museum the ruins of a Medieval castle. The prehistoric city and palace of Cadmus, founder of Thebes, lie on a hill outside the town. Here were found tablets of "Linear B" and seals of the 14th century B.C.

## LEVADIA
## Chaeronia - Orchomenos

**Levadia** is a modern commercial town and stop-over for visitors on their way to Delphi. Everywhere in the centre of the town are restaurants, cafés, and snack bars serving "souvlakia", the town's speciality. Just off the centre, at the foot of a hill and next to a cool stream is a tourist pavilion and open-air restaurants with tables under huge plane trees. Opposite the pavilion is the cave of the famous ancient Oracle of Trophonios.

Above this place, on the top of the hill, is situated the Medieval Castle. The Clock Tower of the town is a gift of Lord Elgin. Levadia produces a rich variety of local handicrafts.

Other towns and places of historical interest in Central Greece are **Chaeronia**, Plutarch's birthplace, and the place where Philip of Macedonia defeated the Athenians in 338 B.C. A colossal stone lion still standing there commemorates the famous battle.

The small museum contains exhibits from the area. Also of interest are the ruins of an ancient theatre below the acropolis of the town.

Not far away from here are the ruins of the Mycenaean fortified town of **Orchomenos** with the dome shaped grave, so called "Treasury of Minyas", its legendary founder.

## Ossios Loukas

Halfway to Delphi from Levadia the road turns to the left and leads to the 11th century **Monastery of Ossios Loukas**. Its Byzantine cathedral Is decorated with splendid mosaics and it Is archltectually one of the finest Byzantine monuments in the country.

The view from the Monastery's terrace is superb, taking in the whole of the green valley below. Most visitors to Delphi like to stop here for refreshments.

## Arachova

Some 6 km before reaching Delphi, coming from Levadia, the road ascends the slopes of Mount Parnassos winding its way through a rugged but magnificent landscape and passes through **Arachova**. This picturesque village clings on a rocky ledge on the slopes of the mountain. Its main street is lined with shops displaying a wide range of local handicrafts, including the well-known «flocati» rugs.

Eastertime is one of the most colourful religious events in Arachova with an open air feast, folk dances and the original contest of the "Race of Old Men" on a slope of Mount Parnassos.

1

2

3

4

The Parnassos Ski Center is accessible from Arachova along a good road (23 kms) which leads to the area of **Fterolakas**. There is an organized Ski Center at an altitude of 1,650-2,000 metres.

## AMPHISSA
## Itea - Galaxidi

At a distance of 21 kms from Delphi is situated **Amphissa** in the middle of one splendid extensive olive grove. It is the capital of the Province of Phokis and has some remains of ancient walls and a ruined Frankish castle.

**Itea** (19 kms from Delphi) is a picturesque port built at the head of the Gulf of Itea, near the ruins of Kirtha, the port of ancient Delphi.

**Galaxidi** is an attractive small seaside town near Itea. It was a rich shipping center of the 17th and 18th centuries.

1. The marble Lion of Chaironeia, which marked the communal grave of the Sacred Band of Thebans that was crushed (338 B.C.) in the battle with Philip B' of Macedonia.
2. Mosaic from the monastery of Ossios Loukas.
3. Monastery of Ossios Loukas.
4. The ski center of Mount Parnassos.
5. Characteristic folk dance with traditional costumes.
6. View of Arachova.

# DELPHI

The grandeur of Delphi has to be seen to be believed. Nature and ancient ruins blend in an extraordinary way enhancing the beauty of one another against a setting of mountains, terraces and trees. Situated at a height of 700 metres and at a distance of 164 kms from Athens, Delphi is impressive in all seasons. It has none of the garish quality and noisiness that are so much a part of popular tourist centres. It is still a village with some very good hotels and restaurants and the usual souvenir shops.

The history of Delphi began when the first mysterious fumes, rising from the earth below the Phaedriades rocks, gave a sacred character to the site. Originally, the place was sacred to Gaea or Themis, the earth goddes. Later, seafarers from Crete introduced the cult of Apollo Delphinius. In time, the mysterious prophecies of its oracle exercised great influence in the ancient world.

The sanctuary of Apollo was surrounded by a wall and within it the sacred site was filled with monuments, statues, and some twenty treasuries—replicas of temples—which housed valuable trophies from wars, archives and treasures. Also in the sanctuary were a small theatre, with a seating capacity of 5,000 and the Temple of Apollo (510 B.C.). In its "Adyton", the "Holy of Holies", Pythia (the High Priestess) sat on a tripod and delivered oracles in a state of intoxication from the fumes emanating from the chasm below. Delphi was consulted on all matters concerning religion, politics, and even individual morality.

Delphi was also the centre of meetings of the Amphictyonic League (the nearest equivalent to the United Nations Organization for the isolated ancient Greek city-states).

Just below the main road and opposite the sanctuary there is a group of ancient ruins called Marmaria, or the Marbles, which consists of the remains of two temples of Athens, and a Tholos, a round Doric temple. There are also traces of the Gymnasium where athletes taking part in the famous Pythian Games trained.

Delphi was plundered and its treasures carried away to adorn the capitals of its invaders, but the final blow came in 385 A.D., when the emperor of Byzantium Theodosius ordered its abolition.

## Museum

The Museum of Delphi contains excellent pieces from the Archaic and Classical periods. Among them the Charioteer, the pediments from the temple of Apollo, the metopes from the treasury of the Sicyonians, the "navel of the earth", the exquisite archaic statues ("Kouroi") of Kleovis and Viton, the Winged Sphinx of the Naxians and the metopes from the treasury of the Athenians, among others. They are all priceless finds that fill the visitor with wonderment and admiration for the art and the civilization that flourished at Delphi.

*1. The bronze statue of the "Charioteer", one of the most famous statues of ancient Greek world (1st quarter of the 5th century BC, Archaeological Museum of Delphi). 2. View of the Temple of Apollo.*

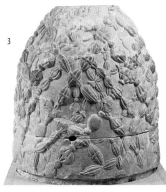

*3. The marble Delphic "Ompalos" that was in front of the Sanctuary of Apollo and symbolized the center of the earth. 4. The Sphinx of the Naxians, dedicated from the Naxians to the Sanctuary of Apollo (570 BC).*

## Kamena Vourla - Thermopylae

On the eastern shores of mainland Greece is situated the hot springs health resort of **Kamena Vourla**. It lies on the edge of a wooded coastline that slopes down to a beautiful beach.

**Thermopylae** is the famous site of the historic battle between the Spartans, led by Leonidas, and the Persian army of Xerxes (480 B.C.). The huge monument to Leonidas and 300 cypress trees commemorate the death of the heroic Spartans.

## LAMIA - Karpenissi

**Lamia** is situated along the National Road to Thessaloniki (214 kms from Athens). It can also be reached from Levadia. It is an important road and rail junction and the starting point for excursions into the mountainous inland regions. Lamia itself is a pleasant town flanked by two pine-clad hills. On the summit of one stands the Medieval fortress of Akrolamia.

The region's favourite resort is **Karpenissi**, in the heart of Roumeli. From Lamia the road twists up the slopes of Mount Tymphristos for some 80 km before reaching this cool and beautiful mountain village surrounded by magnificent scenery and extensive views.

1. View of Kamena Vourla.
2. The monument of Leonidas and his 300 Spartians at Thermopylae.
3. Characteristic folk dance, during the Easter, at Sterea Ellada.
4. Panoramic view of Karpenisi.
5. The Prusso Monastery, in Eurytania..
6. The "Eurytanika tembi", on the way to Prusso.
7. View of the "Kremasti' lake on the way from Agrinio to Karpenissi.

6

7

# 4 euboea

*Euboea is situated along the coast of Boeotia and Attica forming a natural continuation of central Greece. It is 180 kms long and its width varies from 7 to 50 kms. It has a total area (together with its islands) of 3.908 sq. kms and a population of about 210.000.*

*Euboea is largely mountainous, but its few small plains are fertile and the whole island has a plenty of forests and olive groves.*

## CHALKIDA

**Chalkida**, the capital of Euboea (88 kms from Athens), is situated on the Strait of Euripos, famous from ancient times for the phenomenon of the strong tidal current, which flows through the channel at a speed of 4-16 knots, changing direction roughly every 6 hours.

Chalkis was an important and powerful city-state of ancient times and a main strategic town during the Byzantine, the Venetian and Turkish occupations. Now it is a charming town with many ancient and medieval remains.

Every part of Euboea has its own individual charm. Among the most popular sites in the south are:

**Eretria** (23 kms from Chalkis). It is a picturesque small town with interesting ancient remains (a remarkable ancient theatre, a collection of marvellous Eretrian vases in the Museum and others).

**Amarynthos** (8 kms from Eretria). It is a fascinating village in an idyllic bay.

From **Lepoura** (23 kms from Amarynthos) the road turns to north and ends at

the so-called "balcony to the Aegean Sea" **Kymi** near the ruins of Ancient Kymi (the first of the Greek city-states to send colonists to Italy where they founded the city of Naples).

From Lepoura another branch of the road goes south, passes through the beautiful villages **Krieza**, **Styra** (near to the Homeric city Styra), **Marmari** and others and ends at the charming town of **Karystos**, the most southern port of Euboea (128 kms from Chalkis). It has, among others, the famous Venetian castle "Castel Rosso" and it offers the possibilities of reaching the beauties of Mountain Ochi.

*1. Silver stater from Aegina.*
*2. Traditional costume from Agia Anna.*
*3. View of Chalkida, with the bridge.*
*4. Karystos, the Castello Rosso (Red Castle).*
*5. General view of the beach in Nea Styra.*
*6. The island of Dreams or Pezonissi, opposite Eretria.*

Another road leads from Chalkis to the picturesque village **Steni** (33 kms), the starting point for the climb up the Mountain Dirphys (through fantastic forests and ravines).

A wonderful trip can be made to the northwest from Chalkis. **Prokopion**, formerly known as Ahmet Agha is a unique summer resort (58 km from Chalkis) and lying in a valley known to travellers since the days of Lord Byron.

Near Prokopi you can visit the Monastery of Agios Ioannis o Rossos (the Russian), with the relic of the saint that was brought here by the Asia Minor refugees, in 1922.

**Mantoudi** and **Limni** ofer a pleasant combination of landscapes of the mountain and of the sea.

The well-known spa resort **Edipsos** (172 kms from Chalkis) is also connected by ferry boats with Arkitsa and Glyfa. It attracts many visitors mainly in the summertime. They come here to benefit from the health-giving properties of the hot springs and to enjoy a holiday with all modern amenities.

The itinerary north of Chalkis as far as Edipsos is one long perfection, taking the visitor through forest-clad hills and a landscape rich in varied-vegetation - plane trees, oleander, mulberry and walnut trees.

Through **Istiaia** (the ancient Histiaia) the road reaches the Cape Artemission, site of the famous sea battle between the Greek and Persian fleets in 480 B.C.

## SKYROS

**Skyros** (one of the Northern Sporades Islands), across from Kymi, is very interesting. Its small town, called Chora, clambers up the hill in a white half-circle and is dominated by its ancient acropolis, one of the best strongholds in the Aegean. In the Middle Ages it was made into a fortress and there are Byzantine and Venetian ruins to be seen on the site today.

Skyros is famous for its handicrafts and folk arts. Every Skyrian house is a museum in miniature of popular art.

1. View of "Limni" from the sea.
2. The historical spa – hotel "Thermai Sylla" in Aedipsos.
3. View of Aedipsos.
4. The "Poseidon of Artemision", (dated to ca. 460 BC, National Archaeological Museum).
5. Atsitsa beach, at the west side of Skyros.
6. View of the outside of the temple of Agios Ioannis o Rossos (St. John the Russian).
7. Skyros. View of Chora.

# 4 thessaly sporades

Thessaly has the largest plain in Greece, a densely cultivated area ringed round by the Pindus, Othrys, Pelion, Ossa, Olympus and Agrapha mountain ranges. The River Penios meanders across the plain, and to the north it falls through the celebrated Tempi gorge, a narrow pass above which tower the steep slopes of Mt Olympus and Mt Ossa.

Archaeological excavations In this region have disclosed that Thessaly was inhabited 100.000 years ago. Remains of later periods, Old Stone Age and New Stone Age, have been unearthed at Sesklo, Dimini, lolkos and elsewhere in the region. More than 100 prehistoric settlements were discovered in Thessaly.

The inhabitants (3000-1100 B.C.) were called Aiolians, Aimones, Minyes, Boetians, Achaioi, Hellenes, Myrmidones etc. The region of the plain was divided into four districts called Pelasgiotis, Thessaliotis, Estiaiotis and Phthiotis. There were also mountainous districts like Perraivia, Dolopia and Magnesia.

During the Classic period Thessaly tried to be independent from the alliances of other Greek states. It is characteristic that during the Peloponnesian war most of Thessalian cities became rich by selling agricultural products and horses to the Athenians and Spartians

too. In 352 the king of Macedonia, Philip II, occupied Thessaly. In 197 B.C. the region became a district of the Roman state.

During the Byzantine period Thessaly was a separate district and suffered the invasions of barbarians. After the occupation of Constantinople by the Franks, the area was divided in fiefdoms ruled by the nobles. In 1230 it was liberated by the Master of Epirus Theodore. In 1309 it was occupied and ruined by the Catalans and later by the Albanians. In the 14th century Thessaly became a province of the Servians. From the 14th century the Turks tried to occupy it, finally succeeding in 1420.

The liberation of Thessaly from the Turks was effected in 1881 except the province of Elassona which was eventually united in 1912.

## Mount Olympus

This mythical mountain, site of the Palaces of the twelve ancient gods of the Greek mythology, is situated in the northeast of Thessaly. It forms a natural barrier on the road to southern Greece and has been a mountain of great strategic importance from prehistoric times.

Olympus has many towering peaks and imposing gorges. Its slopes offer a fantastic area, suitable for winter sports. From January to mid-March there is usualy snow in abundance at an altitude of 1,500 meters. Many times, during the same period, skiing is possible and pleasant at an altitude of 1,000 meters. The skiers usually aproach from the west, via Elassona, the so-called Lower Olympus, while the mountaineers reach Upper Olympus from the east, via Litochoro.

1. Silver coin of Thessaly depicting a horse.
2. The two higher crests of Olympos, Stephani (2909 m.) on the left and Mytikas (2917 m.) on the right.

## TRIKALA

The capital town of the province after which Trikala is named, stands on the site of ancient Trikki which together with the island of Cos and Epidaurus, was consecrates to Asclepius, the god of medicine. It was also famed for its horses. On the summit of its wooded hill is situated a Byzantine fortress built on the site of the ancient acropolis.

### Kalampaka

This is a fascinating small town built on the site of the ancient city of Aeginion, some 3 kms from Meteora.

## KARDITSA
### "Plastira" lake

Karditsa, the capital of the Prefecture, lies on the west end of the Thessalian plain and consists the commercial and administrative center of the area. Near by, the visitor can admire the famous "Plastira" lake, with the magnificent scenery and the many traditional guesthouses.

## Meteora

**Meteora** is a strange region filled with outcrops of giant rocks in the form of towers and pinnacles, ranging in height from 100 to 150 metres. Once a flourishing monastic community with 24 monasteries, Meteora now has only five occupied monasteries. They were first built in the 14th century by monks seeking isolation and spiritual salvation.

*3. Lithaios, tributary river of Pinios that runs through Trikala.*
*4. View of Plastira Lake.*
*5. Kalambaka.*

The most remarkable features of the monasteries are their domed roofs, wooden galleries, and their upper stories which project precariously over the ladders and net hoists. Today they can be reached without effort along an asphalt road or by narrow stony paths hewn out of the rocks. Of the monasteries that are open to visitors today those of Varlaam, Metamorphosis, Roussanos and Aghios Stephanos are veritable Byzantine museums exhibiting among other things superb icons, old manuscripts and unique mosaics and frescoes.

*1,2. Views of the imposing rocks of Meteora.*
*3. The residence of the Venetian merchant and banker G. Schwarz at Ampelakia, is a museum today.*
*4. The magnificent Tempi Valley.*

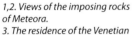

## LARISSA

The enormous region of Thessaly has chosen **Larissa**, an active commercial centre, for its capital town. Progressive and prosperous, Larissa is also a busy junction of routes linking the whole of Central Greece with Epirus, Macedonia and southern Greece. It is built on the site of the ancient city, prehistoric capital of Pelasgians.

Worth visiting are the medieval castle and the archaeological museum.

## Vale of Tempi

Just before the toll post for the Tempi pass a side road leads to **Ambelakia**, a beautiful village, where in 1788 was founded the first internationally known cooperative between capital and labour.

The **Vale of Tempi** is situated 29 kms north of Larissa between Mount Olympus and Mount Ossa (Kissavos). The National Road leading to Thessaloniki goes through this magnificent narrow pass alongside the River Pinios. It is a beautiful route, through some of the finest scenery in all Greece. There is a profusion of green dotted with ivy plants, rhododendrons and plane trees.

The bubbling springs in the vicinity were once dedicated to the goddess Aphrodite. In the Valle of Tempi there was a famous Temple dedicated to the god Apollo, older than that of Delphi.

Casting its shadow over this idyllic setting is the medieval **Castle of Orias**, perched on the top of a high rocky hill.

If you go across the small bridge above Pinios river, you will meet the picturesque

little church of **Agia Paraskevi**. Beside the church there is a small opening in the rock that leads, a few meters ahead, to an underground rivulet, with hallowed waters, according to orthodox tradition. The road continues through the lush green valley of Platamon which marks the entrance to Macedonia and Northern Greece.

## VOLOS - Pelion

Volos is a pleasant provincial town at the head of the Gulf of Pagassae (Pagassitikos). It has two main interests. On the one hand, it is a thriving industrial centre and a commercial port, especially concerned with fruit, and on the other, it is a popular holiday resort with safe bathing and excellent facilities for entertainment and relaxation.

*1. Pinios, the river of Tempi.*
*2. A model of Iasonas' ship, at Volos harbor. 3. View of Volos.*
*4. The small but cosmopolitan port of Afissos. 5. View of Volos.*

Volos museum is exceptionally rich in exhibits, some of which are considered unique. The tombstones are not great artistic value but serve as historical "documents". They are rectangular pieces of marble with pediments as was usual in antiquity.

Of these, twenty have preserved their paintings almost intact.

The main streets of Volos all bear names of Pelion's proud past - Jason, Iolkos, Demetrias. The waterfront is aptly called the quay of the Argonauts. It is here that the town's modern hotels and seafront cafés are situated.

**Mount Pelion** is the celebrated, densely forested abode of the ancient Greek gods and heroes, and the scene of many colourful and dramatic adventures in Greek mythology. Here, Eris set the Golden Apple of Discord rolling at the wedding feast of Peleus. Jason set out with the Argonauts in quest of the Golden Fleece, and the Titans made a futile attempt to pile Pelion on Ossa. Mount Pelion's 24 picturesque villages nestle on the slopes of the mountain, among chestnut trees, olive groves, peach,

apple, and pear orchards. A well-surfaced road follows the cost for some distance before veering inland to begin its steep climb. The distinctive architecture of Pelion's houses is unique: tall buildings with iron doors and small wrought-iron windows on the ground floor. They cling to the mountain side, three-storied in front and single-storied at the back, which is level with the road or pathway.

From its highest peak, called Pourianos Stavros, rising to a height of 1,651 metres, down to its last straggling foothills at Trikeri, Pelion is lush and green.

Starting from Volos and travelling either northwards or eastwards it is an ideal way to see some of Pelion's best known villages, beaches, and beauty spots, among them **Ano Volos**, **Portaria**, **Makrynitsa**, **Hania**, **Zagora**, **Tsangarada**, **Milopotamos** beach, **Milies**, **Argalasti**, **Trikeri**, **Vyzitsa**, **Afissos**, **Kala Nera**, **Aghios Ioannis**, **Kissos**, **Chorefto**.

*1. Makrinista, a mountain settlement, surrounded by trees.*
*2. The ski center of Agriolefkes.*
*3. The beach of Agios Ioannis.*

# SPORADES

The four islands Skyros (see page 65), Skiathos, Skopelos and Alonissos are situated opposite the northern-east coast of Euboea. They are known as the Northern Sporades and all four are accessible from Volos by boat. Life on these islands ambles along at a leisurely pace, offering simple, carefree holidays with time for lazing in the sun, swimming, underwater fishing and skin diving.

**Skiathos** has only one nine-kilometre stretch of road hugging the southern coast with its many lovely bays. It links the town with Koukounaries, the famous stony pine grove and beach. Around Skiathos there are no less than 9 smaller islets. Two of these lie across the main harbour. Skiathos is green, peaceful and idyllic, with a wooded hill rising to 438 metres.

**Skopelos** is gaining in popularity nowadays with those who want a quiet holiday away from the crowds. Apparently, the island was a Cretan colony in prehistoric times and there are a fair number of ruins scattered on its 96 square kilometres. Much of it is cultivated with fruit trees and there are olive trees everywhere.

**Alonissos** has an area of only 62 sq. miles and is oblong, with a precipitous northwestern coastline and hilly interior. It has some small fertile plains but the islanders are mainly occupied with fishing.

*1. Panoramic view of Skiathos.*
*2. The harbor Skopelos.*
*3. General view of the verdant Alonissos.*

*p.74-75*
*"Chrissi Amoudia" at Koukounaries of Skiathos, one of the most beautiful beaches of the country.*
*Inlaid photos: 1.Skiathos has many ruins of buzantine churches. 2. Tradition survives in all of the Sporades islands. 3. The famous Lalaria, one of the most amazing sites of Skiathos.*

3

Epirus, which is Greek for continent, is a superb mountain region covering an area of 9,203 sq. kms in Northwestern Greece. It has a population of 450,000, and its capital town is Ioannina.

Protected in the east by the mighty Pindus range and the serried peaks of Panaetolikon, Epirus is a region with vast orange groves surrounding the deep inlet of the Ambracian Gulf. Some of its most famous towns are **Ioannina, Arta, Parga**, and **Igoumenitsa**.

The well-preserved ruins of polygonal walls, theatre and odeum at Kassopi, in central Epirus, reflect an era in the history of the region when the first of the Greek tribes came to settle here in the Bronze Age. Other interesting ruins include those at Nikopolis, near Preveza, an ancient city built by Octavius when in 31 B.C. he defeated the fleet of Antony and Cleopatra at Actium. Even more impressive is the Theatre of Dodoni, one of the best preserved ancient theatres in Greece.

The serene flow of life in picturesque towns and idyllic valleys, and the fine beaches on the shores of the Ionian Sea combine to attract an everincreasing number of visitors to Epirus, especially now that Igoumenitsa has become a main gate of entry into Greece for motorists arriving from Italy.

From Igoumenitsa an excellent road climbs up 101 kms to Ioannina, where a choice has to be made whether to travel northwards and then eastwards through the splendid scenery of the Pindus range to Metsovo, and over the Katara pass to Meteora, Trikala, Larissa and then on to the Athens-Thessaloniki toll highway. The other choice, which is also the more usual, is to head southwards through Arta, Amphilochia, to Agrinion for the car ferry to Rio, on the Peloponnese.

The fast, new and scenic highway from Igoumenitsa to Rio across from the Peloponnese is one long perfection. It winds up into hills and through woods, past green meadows that are bright and scented with flowers, and into a valley where oleanders grow beside stretches of planetree-shaded river banks. Here one can pitch a tent and spend days by the River Louros, enjoying a swim and pastoral meals by a green bank, with sheep and goat bells tinkling away in the distance.

Apart from the several ancient sites in the region, the Perama Caves with their fascinating underworld of stalactites and stalagmites are also worth a prolonged visit. They are situated 3 kms from Ioannina.

## IOANNINA

Ioannina (or Yiannena) is situated 459 kms from Athens (via Rion-Antirrion) and some 100 kms from Igoumenitsa on the shore of legendary Lake Pamvotis. It is an important commercial and cultural centre, Ioannina was founded by the Emperor Justinian in the 6th century A.D. It rose slowly in statue and by the 13th century it was a flourishing commercial town. Under Turkish occupation in the 18th century it served as a stronghold and seat of Ali Pasha of Tepelini.

To this day Ioannina retains a marked medieval character with its old houses and shops lining narrow streets. It is essentially a historical town, holding on to its traditions which the visitor enjoys together with its modern attractions.

The most interesting feature of Ioannina is the lake which almost surrounds it. Six tiny Byzantine monasteries dot the islands In the lake, and of these the most noteworthy is the 11th century Aghios Nikolaos Dilios with boldly conceived frescoes of "Judas Returning the 30 Pieces of Silver" and the "Last Judgement".

1. Silver drachma of the Epirotians, dated from the Classical period.
2. The bridge of the Voidomatis' river, that runs through Vikos Gorge.
3. The Fethiye Djami (mosque) in Ioannina, which was built in 1430 and consisted the palatial residence of Ali Pasha.
4. The lake of Ioannina, with its island in front of the town.

## Dodoni

Before leaving Ioannina it is worth travelling to the foothills of Mount Tomaros, 22 kms southwest of Ioannina, to visit the site of **Ancient Dodonl**. Remains in the area are those of the ancient oracle, the acropolis, and a few ruins. The theatre dates from the 3rd century B.C. and is used in the summer for performances of ancient Greek Drama during the Dodoni Festival.

## Zagorochoria

A kind of "Grand Canyon" of Europe is the Vikos Ravine (30 kms north of Ioannina) with its 45 idyllic villages known as the **Zagorochoria**, and Voidomati, tributary river of Aoos, that runs through it.

## Metsovo

Metsovo, has a character all its own. It is situated up in the mountains some 60 kms NE of Ioannina, on the slopes of the Pindus range. It is a quaint town and extremely picturesque with many of its inhabitants still wearing their colourful costumes. Lots of the houses are small museums in themselves, displaying as well as producing many of the local handicrafts.

*1. The town of Konitsa, on the slope of the Trapezitsa mountain.*
*2. The Molivdoskepasti Monastery (5th century BC), near Konitsa.*
*3. Old men from Metsovo, wearing traditional costumes.*
*4. The ancient theater of Dodoni.*
*Opposite page: View of Papigo.*

## ARTA - PREVEZA

**Arta** is situated on the River Arachthos and its plain is fertile and intensively cultivated. As early as the 13th century it was the capital of the Despotate of Epirus, a Byzantine principality. Overlooking the town is a medieval fortress. Of interest in Arta is the 18th century bridge which spans the river and the 13th century monastery of Panayia Parigoritissa.

**Preveza** lies on the shores of the Ambracian Gulf and can be reached along the road that branches off to the right before coming into Arta. It is a pretty and peaceful town surrounded by olive groves on one side, while across the narrow stretch of sea lies the island of Lefkas.

**Ancient Nikopolis** is near Preveza. Its surviving remains include the Temples of Poseidon and Ares, the city walls and two theatres.

4   The boat trip along the **Acheron river**, where the Ancient Greeks believed the entrance to Hades lie, is unique and mysterious.

1. The famous "Gefyri tis Artas" (Arta's bridge).
2. The Odeion of ancient Nicopolis, dated from the 1st century AD.
3. The Kipina Monastery, in Christi of Arta.
4. Preveza, the small island of Agia Paraskevi. 5. Preveza, the ancient Nicopolis. 6. The harbor and the city of Preveza.

## IGOUMENITSA
## Syvota - Parga

**Igoumenitsa** is situated at the head of a bay, opposite the island of Corfu (Kerkyra). It is one of the main gateways to Greece and so visitors' comforts are well-looked after by small modern hotels as well as other amenities

The daily car-ferry services from Italy and the many more ferries connecting Corfu with the mainland give life to this attractive little port. Incoming trafic usually heads for Ioannina, but those not in too much of a hurry make a small detour to **Filiate** (20 kms off the highway), a tree-shaded village from where they can continue the climb as far as the picturesque village of Plession.

**Zitsa**, made famous by Lord Byron in his poem

5

"Childe Harold", lies to the left just a few kilometres before Ioannina (alt. 680 metres). It has splendid views.

**Syvota** is a beautiful village by the sea that belongs to the Prefecture of Thesprotia. Because of its landscape and its sandy beaches, attract many tourists in the last years.

**Parga** is an enchanting little seaside town with two superb beaches below the age-old olive groves on the gentle slopes of Mount Pezovolos. It is situated 48 km south of Igoumenitsa but is best reached by steamer.

*1. View of Igoumentitsa.*
*2, 3. The verdant Syvota with the lacy coasts, south of Igoumenitsa.*
*4, 5. The town of Parga with its picturesque islet.*

# 7 Ionian islands

Strung along the shores of Western Greece, the Ionian Islands reveal yet another totally different facet of Greek landscape. Green and luxuriant, they have been for centuries the crossroads between mainland Greece and Western Europe, and as such they were able to develop their own culture, literature, art and music.

**Corfu, Paxi, Lefkada, Cephalonia, Ithaca, Zakynthos** and **Kythira**, known as the "Eptanissa" in Greek, all share a common historical background and offer their visitors an incredible variety of scenery, character and traditions. Geographically, Kythera is not an Ionian island at all, but is counted with the others because for a long time it was ruled with them by Venice.

In ancient time the Ionian Islands were sought after by the mighty city-states of Sparta, Athens and Corinth. And though they joined in the common struggle against the Romans, they finally fell under Roman overlordship together with the rest of Greece. From then onwards they belonged successively to the Byzantines the Turks and the Venetians until 1797 when they were ceded to France. There followed a period of Russian occupation until the French took over once again and ruled from 1807 to 1814, when the islands fell under British rule. They were finally conceded to Greece in 1863 under the Treaty of London.

The Ionian Islands were fortunate enough not to have come for a long time under Turkish rule and so they were able, in spite of the fact that they were not free, to develop remarkable achievements in literature and the arts, especially in painting. In many of the churches and museums of the Ioanian Islands there are works which show, among others, how Greek art would have developed had it not been for the Turkish occupation in the rest of the country. The Ioanian Islands are also the birthplace of many prominent men of letters, among them Andreas Kalvos, Hugo Foscolo, Dionysios Solomos, who wrote the Greek National Anthem, and Aristoteles Valaoritis

1. Silver Corinthian crater depicting Pegasus.
2. View of Pontikonissi and the Church of Our Lady Vlacherna.
3. A walk through the alleyways of the old town.
4. The town of Corfu.

2

## CORFU (KERKYRA)

Corfu is the gateway to Greece for those arriving from Europe. The island has been mentioned by Homer in his «Odyssey». The island's most flourishing period began in 734 B.C., when its first colonists, the Corinthians, arrived here. In the following centuries Corfu shared the fate of the rest of the Ionian Islands. There was a great cultural development during the Venetian and French occupations, when the island boasted a vast library with rare manuscripts and books, a school of art, lyric theatre and several institutions of learning.

**Corfu town** has a strong Venetian character and countless monuments dating from the fifteenth to the late eighteenth century. The Regency Palace with its graceful colonnade reminds us of the British presence on the island as it lines the huge square in the centre of

the town and looks on to the Esplanade, with its profusion of Greek, Venetian and British monuments. To the west, tall arcaded houses, dating from the French domination, line the picturesque street. Also of interest is the 16th century Cathedral dedicated to St Spyridon, the patron Saint of Corfu. A silver casket containing his body is carried through the streets of the town in a procession on feast days.

Outside the town there are a number of interesting spots: **Mandouki, Garitza, Mon Repos** and **Pontikonissi**, where the shipwrecked Ulysses, according to mythology, wandered ashore. The **Achilleion Palace**, an ornate structure built by the Empress Elizabeth of Austria and now turned into a casino. **Vlacherna**, another tiny islet, with its Byzantine Monastery standing between tall cypress trees. **Kanoni** which commands a view over the idyllic bay.

Well known as a warm weather playground and resort for almost a century, Corfu has a great many attractions and diversions in addition to incredible views, golden and secluded sands overhung by wooded mountains and groups of off-shore rocks which look like castles in the sea. Homer was the first to sing its charms as the place where Odysseus was washed ashore and found by Nausicaa, daughter of the ruling king Alcinous. Since the time of Odysseus, however, Corfu has seen a long series of invasions and occupations. Greeks,

Romans, the British, Venetians, the French and even Slavs have, at one time or another, controlled Corfu, together with the rest of the Ionian Islands. An atmosphere rather than an archaeological experience, Corfu's main historical wealth was left behind by the Venetians who ruled from the fifteenth to the late eighteenth century.

1

2

## 3

## PAXI - ANTIPAXI

To the south of Corfu, near the shores of Epirus, are two small islands called Paxi and Antipaxi only 19 sq. kms in area. They have recently been developed into fascinating tourist resorts with comfortable bungalows and fine sandy beaches below the olive groves. Covered with dense subtropical vegetation, they offer a delightful retreat away from the crowds.

1. The Wounded Achilles, marble statue dated from the 1854, at the garden of Achilleio.
2. View of Paliokastritsa.
3. Gaios, the capital of Paxi.
4. The Peroulades, west of Sidari.

## LEFKADA

**Lefkada** is very near the Greek mainland and it can easily be reached from Preveza. The island can be explored at leisure by following a dense network of good roads. It is a mountainous island with several small plains and beautiful beaches. Lefkas shares the same historical background as the rest of the Ionian Islands. Recent excavations at **Nydri** have brought to light several prehistoric remains which prove that the island enjoyed a high standard of civilisation in prehistoric times. Lefkas has not been developed for tourism and for that reason appeals to those who seek a simple holiday by clear blue seas. There are excellent beaches (**Aghios Nikitas**, 27 kms from the town, **Lygia, Nydri, Ai-Yiannis** and **Vassiliki**).

## CEPHALONIA

**Cephalonia** is mountainous, sprawling and pine-covered. It is the largest of the Ionian Islands. Among its many attractions are the Mycenaean tombs, ancient mosaics, and medieval castles. Tourist centres are located among pine-tree groves and next to sandy beaches, bays and headlands. **Argostoli**, the principal town, lies on an inlet deep in Livadi Bay which divides the island into two uneven parts.

*1. The coast facing the mainland, with the Ayia Mavra fortress, are joined to Lefkada by a short bridge.*
*2. Lefkada, the verdant Nydri.*
*3. The enchanting Porto Katsiki, one of the most beautiful beaches on the island.*
*4. The beach of Myrtos, Cephalonia.*

1

2

Completely rebuilt after the devastating earthquakes of 1953, the capital is now a modern town with good hotels and lively entertainment along the waterfront in the evenings.

**Lixouri**, the island's second town on the opposite shore has excellent bathing facilities. Of interest on the island are the villages of **Kastro**, medieval **San Giorgio** which once held 15,000 inhabitants within its ramparts, and the **Mazarakata** excavations made on 83 Mycenaean tombs. Cephalonia is linked to Patras by ferry boat (52 n. miles).

## ITHACA

Ithaca, the famous birthplace of Homer's Ulysses, is mountainous and arid, so its few inhabitants seek work as seamen or else emigrate. Ithaca has countless harbours and coves ideal for swimming, skin-diving and fishing. The **Grotto of the Nymphs**, the island's main tourist attraction, is said to be the cave where Ulysses hid his treasure on his return from the Phaeacians. Ithaca is rich in historical and archaeological finds dating from the peak of the Mycenaean Age (1500-1100 B.C.). A good road crosses the whole island, providing some superb views of the sea on either side.

3

*1. View of Argostoli, the capital of Cephalonia.*
*2. 2. Fiskardo, one of the best-known sites of Cephalonia.*
*3. Panoramic view of Vathi, in Ithaca.*
*4. The astonishing Kaladi at Kythira.*
*5. Skourtis, Zakynthos.*
*6. Panoramic view of the town of Zakynthos.*

4

## KYTHIRA

**Kythira** can be reached from Pireaus, Gythion or Monemvasia. It is one of the seven Ionian islands, the Eptanissa, but geographically it belongs to the Peloponnese since it lies south of the Laconic Gulf. This mythical island of Aphrodite was a Minoan and then a Phoenician colony before belonging to the Lacedaemonians. In the Middle Ages it was a pirate base and then a Venetian colony. The Venetian style can still be seen with the castles and many of the houses.

## ZAKYNTHOS

«Wooded **Zakynthos**» as Homer called the island, is the garden island lying opposite the north-western coast of the Peloponnese. Several times a day, car-ferries ply between Kyllini and Zakynthos. This enchanting island was almost entirely destroyed in the tragic earthquake of 1953. The capital, also called Zakynthos, has been rebuilt in a modification of the original Venetian style houses and spacious squares. Apart from numerous associations and tradition in poets, artists and musicians, the island is rich in natural attractions.

The eastern coast, in the centre of which is situated the town of Zakynthos, is surrounded by a low range of hills, on one of which stands a Venetian citadel and fort, while on the other is the plateau of Akrotiri, with its villas, gardens, orchards and olive groves.

Summer lasts from May to October in Zakynthos, and swimming, yachting and fishing can be enjoyed in a glittering turquoise and emerald sea.

5

6

The famous "Navagio" beach, where the Caretta Caretta turtle reproduces itself.

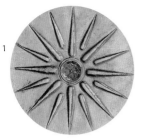

# 8 macedonia

Macedonia, the largest and northrnmost of the 9 Greek Provinces, is bounded on the north by Bulgaria, Yugoslavia and Albania. It possesses great fertile plains, many large rivers like the Nestos, the Aliakmon, the Strymon and the Axios, and several lakes. While the climate along the coast is Mediterranean, further inland it is continental. The archaeological digs which have taken place at Olynthos, Servia and elsewhere show that Macedonia was inhabited in the Neolithic period, while the recent discovery of a human skull of the Neanderthal type in the Petralona cave, Halkidiki (see below) indicates that there was a human presence in the area in much earlier times.

Macedonia was an important part of ancient Greece, with a history of more than 3,000 years. This is proved by finds from the Mycenean period (before 1100 BC) and the Geometric period (1000 BC), and above all by recent excavations at Vergina, which have brought to light the superb royal tombs of Philip of Macedon (see Veria -Vergina).

The language, religion, customs and way of life of Macedonia were from the very earliest times identical to those of the rest of Greece. Aristotle, the great ancient philosopher, was born and brought up in Macedonia and, of course, spoke Greek. The twelve gods of Olympus, of whom Zeus was the chief, were worshipped by the ancient Macedonians as they were by the Greeks throughout the ancient Greek world.

Philip II (357-366 B.C.) founded Macedonian greatness and eventually succeeded in extending his dominion by conquering southern Greece. After his assassination he was succeeded by his son Alexander III, better known as Alexander the Great, a military and political genius who pushed the frontiers of his kingdom deep into Asia, subduing a host of peoples as he went along.

After the Romans defeated King Perseus at Pydna (168 B.C.), they became masters of Macedonia and its decline was very rapid. During the Byzantine era, it became one of the most important provinces of the Empire.

Unter Turkish rule, after the 15th century, Macedonia retained its importance as a region of agricultural and commercial activities. During the Turkish occupation the Macedonians often tried to liberate their country. Their efforts intensified in the years of the 1821 Greek Revolution against the Turks. Macedonia was incorporated into Greece after the 1st world war.

1. The star of Vergina.
2. The statue of Alexander the Great on the seafront at Thessaloniki.

# THESSALONIKI

**Thessaloniki**, the capital of Northern Greece, is the second Greek city of importance after Athens. With the establishment in recent years of many factories, it has experienced an amazing economic and industrial growth. Moreover, it is an important cultural centre as well. It possesses one of the biggest Balkan universities, a Teaching Academy, the Ecumenic Institute, two State Schools of Music, and several Cultural Societies.

Thessaloniki was founded by Cassander, King of Macedonia (315 B.C.), who named the new city after his wife, Thessaloniki Alexander the Great's sister. It was the favourite city of the Macedonian Kings, its popularity continuing even after Macedonia became a Roman province in 148 B.C. Much later, in the Byzantine era, it was the second most important city of the Empire, after Constantinople.

Byzantine chronicles refer to it as «the most splendid and proudest city», «the Reigning City», and «the populous City», for Thessaloniki was not only the cultural and political centre of the Byzantine Empire. It also remained for centuries the uncaptured citadel, successfully repulsing wave after wave of attacks by different barbaric hordes.

The medieval monuments which remain in Thessaloniki today testify to its former splendour and truly great prosperity.

The following are worth visiting: The **Archaeological Museum** with its numerous

interesting exhibits of the Classical and Roman periods, including the «Dervenion Crater». The **Church of Saint Demetrius** (the city's patron saint), a five-naved basilica, built over the Saint's tomb in the 5th century A.D., is one of the most superb monuments of the Greek Orthodox tradition. Besides its architectural worth and the wealth of its carvings, its mosaics, which cover a period dating from the 6th to the 9th century A.D., are especially remarkable. The **Rotonda**, another noteworthy monument is a circular building erected in 306 A.D. In the reign of Theodossius the Great it was turned into a Christian church. The mosaics embellishing its arches and the imposing dome belong to this later period.

4

Other interesting churches are «**Acheiropoietos**» (not made by hand), one of the best examples of the ancient Greek Christian basilica style (5tn century); the Church of **Panaghia Chalkeon** (Holy Virgin of the Coppersmiths, (11th century); the Church of **Aghia Sophia**, an early domed basilica (6th century) with splendid mosaics; the Church of **Twelve Apostles** (13th century) with special ornamental brickwork; the **Monastery of Vlatadon** with a small chapel of cruciform type (14th century). There are also the medieval walls of the town and the triumphal **Arch of the Emperor Galerius** on the Via Egnatia built in 303 A.D. The Venetian **White Tower**, the Thessaloniki's prominent landmark, was built in the 15th century.

5

Thessaloniki also has a number of country places for rest and leisure: **Aghia Triada,** 25 km out of town is a wooded seaside district; **Nea Mechaniona**, a lovely holiday resort offering a fine beach and plenty of fresh fish. **Panorama, Asvestohori** and **Hortiati** are mountain resorts.

6

*1. Byzantine mosaic in the Church of Saint Demetrius.*
*2. Aristotelous square, Thessaloniki.*
*3. The White Tower.*
*4. The Arch of Galerius or "Kamara".*
*5. The Rotonda, 4th century AC.*
*6. Main street at "Ladadika".*

## KATERINI - Dion

**Katerini**, capital of the Prefecture of Pieria, stands on the plain between Mt Olympus of the myths and the Pieria mountains, 75 km from Thessaloniki and 6 km from the sea. It is a relatively new town. Nearby are the fine beaches of Methoni, Makriyalos, Olympiaki Akti, Plaka Litochorou and, best of all, Platamonas.

The outstanding archaeological site of **Dion** is 20 km from the town and has produced finds of the greatest value. Recent excavations have laid bare sanctuaries, tombs, theatres, a basilica and other buildings covering the period from the early iron Age (1100 BC) to the Byzantine age. Dion, beneath the awe-inspiring peaks of Olympus, was an important cult site for the Macedonians - rather along the lines of Delphi and Olympia.

To the south of Katerini is **Litochoro**, a pretty village which is the starting-point for the ascent of Mt Olympus, the highest mountain in Greece.

## Platamonas

Platamonas is a coastal village, the most popular tourist destination of the area. Built in a verdant landscape that leads right to the sea, it is specially known for the medieval castle that rises above a hill in the foothill of Olympus, in the location where ancient Hirakleia was built.

1. The beach of Katerini.
2. To Litochoro.
3. The Platamonas' castle, dated from the middle Byzantine period (10th century AC) and built to the foothill of Olympus.
4. The archaeological site of Dion.

# VERIA - Vergina

**Veria**, one of the most ancient of Macedonian cities, can boast of several Byzantine churches. Of even greater interest are the tomb of the Macedonian king Philip II, the palace and other archaeological finds recently discovered at the site of **ancient Vergina** (11 kms south-east of Veria), the most momentous archaeological event in recent years. It was populated during the early Iron era, according to the cemetery that was found there, but bloomed during the Archaic and Classical era, when Vergina was the headquarters of Macedonian Kings and a place where famous priests were gathered.

    **Naoussa** is a picturesque town at a distance of 94 km from Thessaloniki. It is well-known for the beautiful textiles its factories turn out, and also for its excellent wine. There are annual carnival festivities held there, among them the «Bula» dance, an interesting local folk event. It has lovely holiday resorts both in summer and in winter, when winter sports enthusiasts meet on Mount Vermion. The village **Seli** (18 km from Naoussa at an altitude of 1,420 m.) is Mount Vermion's ski centre, with skiing facilities and hotels.

*1. The Monastery of Panayia Soumela.*
*2. Panoramic view of Veria.*
*3. View of the archaeological site of Vergina.*
*4. The gold larnax with its outstanding relief and the star with sixteen radii, which was the emplem of the Macedonian dynasty. In the larnax the bones of Phillip II, king of Macedon were found (Archaeological Museum of Thessaloniki).*

## KOZANI - Siatista

A crossroads between Western Macedonia, Epirus, Thessaly and Central Macedonia is Kozani, an historic town, and a commercial and industrial centre.

Its Library posseses thousands of rare and precious manuscripts and other written documents. It is considered to be the second important library in Greece after the Athens National Library.

**Siatista** (25 km west of Kozani) is a picturesque medieval town with large traditional buildings ("archontika") and some interesting Byzantine churches.

## EDESSA - Pella

**Edessa**, the capital town of the district of Pella, is situated on the foothills of Mount Vermion. It is known for its beautiful waterfalls and lies in a sea of green orchards.

According to one legend, the first capital of the ancient Macedonian kings lay in the district of Edessa, at **Aiges**. Then in the 5th century B.C., King Archelaos transferred his capital to Pella, whose ruins have been discovered at a distance of 10 kms outside the picturesque town of Yannitsa.

In the archaeological area of **Pella**, where systematic excavations have been going on in recent years, a few interesting buildings stand out: The most important is that which contains the wonderful mosaic depisting a lion-hunt. That and another mosaic representing a deer are remarkable for the wealth of detail.

## KASTORIA

**Kastoria** is famous for its fur industry. At one time in its past it was a prominent Byzantine centre and has now a number of beautiful churches dating from the 11th to the 18th century to show for it.

The most interesting are the churches of Panaghia Koumbelidiki, Aghioi Anargyroi and Taxiarchai (all of them of the 11th century). Kastoria, also has beautiful old mansions ("Archontika"). The town is built beside the charming **Lake Orestias** (or Lake of Kastoria).

*1. Karanos, the most imposing waterfall of Edessa.*
*2. Mosaic of a lion hunt (4th century BC, Archaeological Museum of Pella).*
*3. Panoramic view of Kozani, the commercial and administrative center of west Macedonia.*
*4. View of the Museum of Kozani*
*5. Interior view of the Folk Museum of Kastoria.*
*6. Panoramic view of the town of Kastoria.*

### FLORINA - Prespa Lakes (Great and Small)

**Florina** is a commercial centre charming (161 km west of Thessaloniki and only 18 km from the frontier post of Nike on the Yugoslav border.

Near Florina (22 km) is the mountain refuge of **Pissoderi**, starting point for skiers and mountaineers.

Two lakes, the **Megali (Great)** and the **Mikri (Small)** Prespa, near Florina, form part of the borders between Greece, Albania and Yugoslavia. Its landscape is beautiful. On the small islet of **Aghios Achilleios** is a very old Byzantine church. Nearby have been discovered remains of an ancient Macedonian settlement.

### GREVENA

Grevena, the capital of the homonymous Prefecture is built 534 meters high, at the west side of Aliakmonas. Gremvotikos, tributary river of Aliakmonas, runs through it. Having more than 10,000 inhabitants, Grevena is the administrative, commercial and cultural center of the area.

## KILKIS

Kilkis, the capital of the homonymous Prefecture is a town with 20,000 inhabitants, built around the hill of Agios Georgios. At the top of the hill stands the church of Agios Georgios, dated from 1832. In Kilkis took place a battle between the Greek and Bulgarian forces during the Second Balcanic War. The Bulgarians left the city after 3 days in June of 1913. .

1. From the plantation of Prespa Lake: "Lefkotsiknias" and panoramic view of the lake.
2. General view of the town of Grevena.
3. Panoramic view of Kilkis.
4. Ruins from the church of Agios Achilleios (990 AC), at the homonymous island of the lake Mikri Prespa.
5. The ski center of Vasilitsa, at the north-west end of the Prefecture of Grevena, 1800 to 2060 meters high.

# SERRES

**Serres**, one of the largest Macedonian towns centre of the tobacco, cotton and cereals trade preserves many monuments of its long history. The most interesting are the Byzantine City Wall on its acropolis, the Byzantine church of Saint Nikolas, and the old Cathedral - Aghioi Theodoroi. Starting from Serres one can go on an excursion to **Amphipolis**, with its famous lion; to **Kerdylia** and its lovely coast, and lastly to **Nigrita**, with its famous mineral springs.

*1. Panoramic view of Drama from Sidirokastro and the fort walls.*
*2. Idyllic view of Lake Kerkini, important biotope of Northern Greece.*
*3. Central square of Drama with the Agia Varvara Springs.*

## DRAMA - Philippi

**Drama** is the chief town of the province by the same name. Having abundant waters, its verdure is very lush. The town, spread out on a fertile plain, is a tobacco growing centre.

**Philippi** is only 25 km away from Drama. An important ancient city, it was built by Philip II, King of Macedonia, in 358 B.C. Some of its remains are the ancient theatre, the Agora, the acropolis, a Sanctuary of Egyptian Deities and others.

In 42 B.C. the famous battle between the forces of Brutus and Cassius on the one hand and those of Octavius. later Emperor Augustus, took place here at Philippi.

In summer ancient Greek plays are staged at the theatre.

*4. Remains at the archaeological site of Philippi.*

## KAVALA

**Kavala** is an affluent town ith a large harbour and modern buildings. Points of interest in it are the **house of Mohammed Ali**, founder of the Egyptian dynasty; the castle walls; the famous **Imaret**, the church of the **Holy Virgin**, and Saint Syllas' Church. There is also a museum which houses significant archaeological finds from eastern Macedonia and Thrace. Kavala also has lovely beaches at **Nea Heraclitsa, Nea Peramos, Periyali, Aspri Ammos**, and **Keramoti**.

1. The famous Kamares, 1550.
2. Panoramic view of Eleftheroupoli, which was a center of processing tobacco.
3. Panoramic view of Kavala.
4. Limenas, Thassos.
5. Chrissi Amoudia beach, Thassos.
6. View of Limenaria by night.

# THASOS

Taking the ferry-boat from Keramoti one can cross to the green island of Thassos, a natural paradise. It is the northernmost Aegean island and a first class tourist centre. The island's economy rests on its timber and the export of lead, iron and antimony. The oil deposits discovered in the nearby region of Prinos now afford opportunities for considerable exploitation.

Almost the whole of Thassos is one vast museum with rich collections of relics dating from its heyday in Classical times.

The archaeological excavations have brought in light the ancient Agora, a theatre, ancient settlement, the commercial port, the city walls, the acropolis, Pan's Sanctuary and many other interesting remains. The large number of monuments attests to the great prosperity of ancient Thassos, which made it the apple of discord between the city-states of Athens and Sparta. Among the great men of Thassos were the painter Polygnotos and the writer Androsthenis who follwd Alexander the Great in his campaigns. The most interesting remains of ancient times are the theatre (originally built in the 4th century), the acropolis, the Agora, the Sanctuaries of Poseidon and Dionysos and others. In the museum one can see fine specimens of Ancient and Archaic art.

The capital of the island (**Limin** or **Thasos**) and the seaside and inland villages are picturesque and quiet.

# CHALKIDIKI

To the southeast of Thessaloniki lies the Chalkidiki peninsula. Of late years, this region has become a Mecca for tourists, with its endless quiet sandy beaches, pine-trees and pretty hamlets. The most interesting part of Chalkidiki is its eastern promontory, Mout Athos, known as Aghion Oros.

The peninsula of Chalkidiki with its three branches, **Kassandras**, **Sithonias** and **Mount Athos** (Aghion Oros), is one of the most picturesque Greek districts. It combines mountainous and insular characteristics and offers an opportunity for a unique experience in the monastic region of Mount Athos.

Apart from Mount Athos, the visitor to Chalkidiki should not miss the following: in the capital town of **Polyghiros**, the **Church of Saint Nicholas**; at **Arnea** the remains of the ancient acropolis; at **Ierissos** the Byzantine tower; at **Kallithea** the tempel of Ammon Zeus; at **Nea Olynthos** the neolithic settlement; at **Ouranoupolis** the Byzantine tower; near **Petralona** the famous Cave known as "Kokkines Petres" (Red Stones) with very interesting fossils

1. The statue of Aeristotele at Stageira.
2. Traditional house in Galatista.
3. Representation of the life of the "oldest" Greek (Homo Neadertal).
4. Mosaic from a house of ancient Olynth, with Pigasos and Vellefonti as the main theme.
5. The beautiful Vourvourou beach in Sithonia. In the background, you can see the Mount Athos.
6. The Glarokavos beach.
7. Nea Potidaia and the canal of the peninsula of Kassandra.

<sup>1</sup> and petrified bones of animals and Neanderthal or Pre-Neanderthal man; at **Kassandra** the small channel.

1. The tower of Fokea.
2. 2. The beach of Kallithea.
3. The "Despoina" (Lady) of Stratoni, woman's marble statue dated from the 1st century AC, Archaological Museum of Polyghiros.
4. Panoramic view of Stratoni.

# AGHION OROS

Its monasteries, despite disasters suffered at various times in its 1000-year old history, still retain a prodigious collection of manuscripts, so that they can be considered a priceless cluster of Byzantine museums. Some of them are still occupied. Mount Athos is also the best example of the development of Byzantine architecture and painting. Architecturally, its churches belong to the category of which prevailed in the churches on the Meteora and in the Peloponnese as well. The numerous murals and the icons in the churches of Mount Athos are of the utmost importance in the study of Byzantine painting. Mount Athos is a peculiar autonomous monastic republic with an exclusively male population. The entry and stay of women is strictly prohibited.

*1. The small harbor of Ouranoupolis, passage to the Mount Athos, with the "Prosforios" tower.*
*2. Monastery of Megisti Lavra.*
*3. Agios Nikolaos of 17th century, from Stavronikita Monastery.*
*4. Monastery of Ayiou Dionysiou.*

# 9 thrace

Thrace is mostly mountainous, and was first inhabitied by Pelasgians, a race closely connected to the other Greek tribes. Thracians founded Eleusis in Attica and the mythical musicians Orpheus and Mousaios were from Thrace. In ancient times, Thrace stretched from Mt. Olympus in the south to the Danube in the north, and among its most famous cities was Abdera, birthplace of Democritos.

Thrace continued to play an important role in history during both the Roman and the Byzantine periods.

A large section of Thrace was ceded to Bulgaria at the beginning of this century, while Turkey took another part after the First World War (Treaty of Lausanne, 1923), while Greece was left with the Xanthi, Komotini and Evros regions, the river Evros acting as a border to the East.

Thrace is largely agricultural, with around 350,000 inhabitants, of both Greek and Muslim origin. It is the most north-easterly part of the Greek state.

1. Bust of the Thracian philosopher Democritos.
2. Waterfall of Leivaditis, at the north of the Prefecture of Xanthi.

Left: Mount Athos, the Monastery of Agios Panteleimonas.

## XANTHI

**Xanthi** lies at the foot of Mount Rodopi (219 km from Thessaloniki) and preserves many of its old traditional houses, as well as its castle on the top of the hills which shelter the town from the north winds.

It is the capital of the Prefecture of Rhodope and an important centre of production and trade of tobacco. 25 km away are the ruins of **Abdera**, the birthplace not only of Democritos, father of atomic science, but also of Protagoras the Sophist, Nikaenetos the poet, Anaxarchos the philosopher and Hecateos the historian, among other famous men. At the site of the ancient city have been found remains of the walls and of a big building with some 26 rooms.

## KOMOTINI

The town of Komotini is situated at a distance of 57 km from Xanthi. It is built almost the middle of a fertile plain, close to the famous Via Egnatia of ancient times, at the foot of Mount Rhodope. It has, among other things, interesting museums (**Archaeological, Folk Art** and **Byzantine ecclesiastic**). Komotini is a lively commercial centre and **Porto Lago** (34 km. southwest) is its sea outlet.

**Porto Lago** is situated on a narrow strip of land between the Gulf of Vistoni and the Vistoni Lagoon. Its area is famous for the water-fowl, fish and eels.

*1. Events of the carnival of Xanthi.*
*2. Panoramic view of Xanthi.*
*3. Alleyways in Komotini.*
*4. Porto Lagos with the chapel of Ayios Nikolaos.*

# ALEXANDROUPOLIS

**Alexandroupolis** (341 km from Thessaloniki via Amphipolis) is one of the new towns of Greece, and its most easterly port in the north. Its visitors enjoy modern amenities, such as comfortable hotels, camping sites, good restaurants and sandy beaches. Alexandroupolis is the capital of the Prefecture of Evros, and the last important town of Greece before reaching the Turkish border. Its area is abounding in game-birds and especially in water-fowl and migratory birds. So it attracts many sportsmen every hunting period.

*1. View of Alexandroupoli.*
*2. Didymoteicho is surrounded by two identical walls that named the city.*
*3. Alexandroupolis' beach with its lighthouse that rise above the coastal road.*

*Opposite: View of the Nestos river, important biotope of Thrace.*

# 10 northeastern aegean islands

*The Northeastern Aegean islands can be counted: the Samothrace, the Limnos, the Lesvos, the Chios, the Samos and the Ikaria.*

## SAMOTHRACE

By taking a small ship or the ferry-boat one can go over Samothrace, the island with the landscapes and tempestuous history. Archaeological excavations have yielded important finds, chief of which is the statue of the "Victory of Samothrace" exhibited today in the Louvre Museum in Paris.

*1. "Sixth from electron", coin from Lesvos.*
*2. The waterfall of "Fonias", Samothrace.*
*3. The sanctuary of the Cabeiri.*
*4,5,6. Views of Myrina, Limnos' capital.*
*7. The Nike of Samothrace, a famous statue thought to have been commissioned to commemorate a naval victory of the Rhodians about 200 BC (Louvre Museum, Paris).*

## LIMNOS

Administratively, Limnos belongs to the district of Lesvos. It has an area of 477 sq km and is situated in the South Thracian sea between Chalkidiki and the Turkish coast. It boasts a pleasant dry climate, a lot of greenery and sandy beaches. The chief town of the island is **Myrina**, or **Castro**. Another interesting little town is **Mudros** with its large port and important commercial activity. Four superimposed prehistoric settlements have been discovered at the site of ancient **Droscopos** on the east coast. Remarkable are also the remains of the two famous ancient cities **Hephaestia** and **Kabeirion**.

# LESVOS

Lesvos, also called Mytilini, is the third largest Greek island after Crete and Euboea. The island is covered with olive groves, orchards and pine forests. In ancient times Lesvos enjoyed a golden age of cultural greatness. Many of its sons and daughters were worthy rivals of the literary giants of the other cities of Greece. Even a summary of their works would take up too much space and time. Therefore, we shall mention only Alcaics, Arion, Terpandros, Errina and the renowned Sappho.

A trip along the lovely coast and to the picturesque hamlets is fantastic. Among the seaside resorts, where one can find coolness and peace during the hot summer months are: **Vigla, Makris Yalos, Tsamakia** with its big pine wood. The hot mineral springs of Lesvos are renowned. They combine the healing properties of the waters with matchless natural surroundings. **Methimna, Plomari** and **Ayiassos** are the prettiest little towns in Lesvos.

The island's chief town, Mytilini, is a brisk place with food future prospects and great literary tradition. Exhibitions are held regularly showing works by local dance troupes. A well-stocked archaeological museum houses the finds of excavations in the island, and the local picture gallery contains some of the works of the famous folk artist Theophilos.

1. Petra.
2. The Petrified Forest.
3. Plomari.

Opposite :
Above: Mytilini.
In the middle: the beach of Eressos.
Below: view of the town of Mytilini.

## SAMOS

Samos, birthplace of the great philosopher and mathematician Pythagoras, is a place where the ancient intellect and culture shone brightly. The island knew the height of its greatness under its ruler Polycrates.

The chief town of the island is Samos, formerly **Vathy**. It has an interesting archaeological museum with finds from the excavations of the Heraion (Goddess Hera's Temple) and the ancient city of Samos. The towns **Pythagorion** and **Carlovassi** (the second town of importance) are worth visiting. The island has also many seaside and mountainous fascinating villages. Unique in Greece is the paleontological museum of the village Mytilinii.

## IKARIA

Ikaria has been nick-named the «radium island» because of its natural radium healing springs. The chief town is **Aghios Kirykos**. Not far away is the spa **Therma**, with modern installations and hotels with all amenities.

*1. Vathy, capital of Samos.*
*2. Agios Kirykos, Ikaria.*
*3. Eydilos, Ikaria.*
*4. "Ikarus fall", roman sarcophagus.*
*Opposite:*
*Above: The statue of Pythagoras in the harbour of Pythagorion.*
*Pythagorion, a place of archaeological and historical interest.*
*Below: Houses on the bay of Kokari.*

# CHIOS

The history of Chios goes back to legendary times. Its first inhabitants were Pelasgians, then Cretans and perhaps Carians and Leleges lived there too. During historical times, Ionians from the Asia Minor coast arrived, and soon turned Chios into a flourishing commercial, artistic, and literary centre, until it was taken by the Persians in 498 B.C. It regained its independence after the sea battle of Mykale.

Places worth visiting are: in Chios town—the ancient city walls, the ancient theatre, the castle, the **Archaeological Museum**, the **Arghention Folk Art Museum**, the **Picture Gallery**.

Outside the town: the famous convent of **Nea Moni** (with an octagonal Byzantine church of the 11th century decorated with splendid mosaics); the picturesque medieval little town of **Pyrghi**; many fascinating little towns and villages (**Vrondados, Kardamyla, Volissos, Karyes**, the area of the villages of the mastic production, **Kalamoti, Mesta** and others).

Near to Chios are situated the small interesting islands of **Oinousses** and **Psara**. Psara played a heroic role during the Greek Revolution of 1821.

1. Pyrgi, the medieval village, Chios.
2. The village of Anavatos, Chios.
3. Oinousses, the five islets near the north-east coast of Chios.

Opposite: Four drachmas, coin from Rhodes representing the head of God Helios.
Mandraki Harbour. The entrance and the fort of St. Nicholas.

# 11 dodecanese

*This group of islands has been called the Dodecanese (12 islands) because the main ones are twelve in number: Patmos, Kalymnos, Leros, Kos, Nisyros, Astypalaea, Tilos, Symi, Chalki, Karpathos, Kasos, Rhodes and Castellorizo.*

## RHODES

Rhodes with its constant sunshine, its antiquities and its incomparable landscapes, make it one of the best known tourist islands in the world. One could call Rhodes «one vast sculptor's studio», since besides the gigantic statue of the Colossus, one of the 7 wonders of the ancient world, there were 3,000 more statues embellishing the island.

In the Classical period Rhodes was a powerful and rich island, exerting influence far and wide. Its second great period was when the island was occupied by the Knights of the Order of Jerusalem (1309-1522). In 1522 Rhodes was conquered by the Turks, followed by the Italians in 1912. In 1947 Rhodes and the other islands of the Dodecanese were incorporated to Greece.

The capital town Rhodes has a quarter of old houses, narrow streets and small stores under the medieval walls, as well as a new part with modern buildings, hotels, shops and facilities. In the town the visitor should not miss: the **Archaeological Museum** containing unique

pieces of Rhodean art; the **Palace of the Grand Master**; the walls of the Castle; the Street of the Knights; and, on the acropolis of ancient Rhodes, the ruins of temples, a theatre, a gymnasium, a stadium and other buildings.

The most interesting places to visit are: Rhodini Park, Kallithea, the Valley of the Butterflies, the Seven Springs, Philerimos, Camiros and the unparalleled Lindos.

**Rhodini Park** (3 km south of the town) is a pleasant place with fountains, ponds, flowers and trees.

**Kallithea** (11 km south-east of the town) is a fully equiped spa and a lovely seaside resort.

**The Valley of Petaloudes** (Butterflies), 26 km from the town, near the village of Kalamiona, offers the magnificent sight of thousands butterflies rising in clouds from trees and bushes in June, July and August.

**Seven Springs** is a beautiful resort with a lake, little waterfalls and many plane-trees.

**Mount Philerimos** (15 km south-west of the town) is an interesting spot with a Byzantine monastery and the remains of a Temple of Athena and of the **ancient city of Ialissos**.

1. Mandraki; in the background the Palace of the Grand Master.
2. The Faliraki beach.
3. Representation of Rhodes Kolissos.
4. The marble statue of Aphrodite of Rhodes (1st century BC, Rhodes Archaeological Museum).
Opposite, above: The Road of the Knights, in the Old City of Rhodes.
Below: Part of the new and old cities of Rhodes.

On the slopes of a hill some 36 km south-west of the town is situated **Kamiros**, the so-called "Pompeii of Rhodes". One can see there the remains of the third of the most ancient towns of the island.

**Lindos** (56 km from the town) combines a picturesque village with lovely beaches under the remains of the impressive ancient acropolis and fortifications built by the Knights and the Turks.

*1. The small harbor of Agios Pavlos. It is said that Apostle Paul disembarked here when he came to Rhodes.*
*2. The cathedral of Panayia Monastery at Filerimo.*
*Opposite page: the Lindos fortress.*

## NISYROS

According to legend, Nisyros, which lies at the centre of the Dodecanese group, was formed when Poseidon broke a piece of rock off Kos and hurled it at the Giant Polybotes. The Carians were the first inhabitants of the island, which, during the classical period, was independent. It continued to be . a free island all the way through the Byzantine Empire, until it was destroyed by the Turks in 1457, after which it remained uninhabited for quite a long time. Nisyros is thickly-wooded, and has many places of interest, among them the volcano. Also worth seeing are the **acropolis**, the **Knights' Castle**, the **Byzantine castle** and the **Stavros monastery**. There are many fine beaches.

## TILOS

Tilos was first peopled by Pelasgians, and the first Dorians arrived on the island about 1100 B.C. The tyrants of Syracuse, Gelon and Ieron, were from here. The capital of the island is called **Megalo Chorio**, and above it stands a castle.

4

5

6 ## CHALKI

Chalki is an isle of unusual beauty situated close
to the southern shores of Rhodes. The island's
name derives from the bronze laboratories it
possessed in antiquity.

## SYMI

This island lies NW of Rhodes. Its capital town Symi
is built tier-fashion below an impressive medieval
castle, situated on the ancient acropolis.

*1. Nisyros, Mandraki castle, and Our Lady "Spiliani.*
*2. "Kratiras", the volcano in Nisyros that last exploded in 1888.*
*3. View of Tilos.*
*4. Chalki's harbor.*
*5. The Panormitis Monastery, in Symi.*
*6. The harbor of Symi.*

## KOS

The island is best known as the birthplace of Hippocrates, the father of medicine. Like Rhodes, it has a superb climate and beautiful scenery. Antiquity has also left traces of a prosperous past. Notable remains of the Classical and the successive periods lie scattered all over Kos. The monuments and places one should not miss seeing are: the **castle** above the harbour; the **Roman Odeum**; the plane-tree under which Hippocrates taught his pupils, so tradition tells us; and a little beyond the town, some 4 km away, the famous **Asklepieion** of Kos, the sanctuary of Asklepios, god of Medicine. Ancient Kos was also well known as birthplace of Apelles, a famous painter of the 4th century B.C.

Medicinal springs are situated with modern facilities south of the town of Kos, on the slopes of the mountain.

1. The Castle of the Knights in Kos town.
2. 2. Panoramic view of the town of Kos.
3. Statue of Hippocrates.
4. The ruins of the basilica of St. Stephen, with the islet of Kastri in the centre of the bay.
5. The Asklepeio and the temple of Apollo on the second level.
6. Kardamaina beach.

3

4

5

## KALYMNOS

**Kalymnos** is one of the more picturesque Dodecanese islands. It is hilly and not very fertile. The main occupation of its inhabitants is sponge diving. They are considered the best divers in the world. Before their boats set out in spring from the capital town Pothia or Kalymnos for the coast of Nord Africa, there are revelries and feasts with interesting popular events.

Relics of prehistoric times were discovered in a cave of a hill called **Aghia Varvara**. The island has also remains of Mycenaean period. There are also remains of a sunken ancient city at Telendos, a small isle near Kalymnos.

## LEROS

Leros, which lies between Patmos and Kalymnos, is the ancient isle of Artemis. It is a pleasant island, full of historical sites and good places for holiday-making. Above the traditional settlement of **Ayia Marina**, the island's capital, rises the **castle of Panayia**, which is still in good condition. Inside the castle is the **church of the Virgin**, with many interesting remains. There is an early Christian church at **Alinda**, and the port of Lakki has a Byzantine church of St. John. At **Paleokastro**, on the way to **Xirokambos**, is the first ancient castle on the island.

*1-2. The beach and the harbor of Kalymnos.*
*3. Agia Marina, Leros.*
*4. Fresco of the Apocalypse, in Patmos.*
*5. The icon of Agios Ioannis Theologos.*
*6. the Agios Ioannis Theologos Monastery.*
*7. General view of Patmos.*

## PATMOS

Patmos is a rocky barren island which must have been practically unknown in ancient times since it is very rarely mentioned by ancient writers. The Romans turned it into a of exile. Here, Saint John spent some time in exile and during his stay in a cave he wrote his «Book of Apocalypse». The monastery of Saint John is a realy interesting museum of Byzantine art and Christian tradition. Many of its manuscripts are famous the world over.

## KARPATHOS

This island lies between Rhodes and Kassos. With its cool climate, dreamlike coastline and strong traditional ties, Karpathos fascinates the visitors who flood its shores in summer. One of its charms is the local Spong Divers Festival in late spring, when strangers to the island are invited to sit with the locals at a communal table and later join in the folk dances to the accompaniment of folk music. Its houses are built in the unique Karpathian tradition. On this island old customs and traditions are faithfully kept up. Even the island costume is something most of the islanders wear every day.

Karpathos is none other than the island known in ancient times as Tetrapolis. Its first inhabitants were Pelasgians, followed by Dorians. Its later history is similar to that of the other islands of the Dodecanese. In the village **Olympus** or **Elympos**, life has retained its traditional colour; the inhabitants wear traditional clothing, and their houses are hundreds of years old. All the major religious festivals are celebrated with Byzantine pomp, and many ancient customs live on.

1. The Kyra-Panaghia beach.
2. The harbor of Karpathos.
3. Olympus or Elympos, in Karpathos; a village that preserves the topical traditions.
4. View of Kasos island.
5. The beautiful Castellorizo.
6. Astypalaea, with its famous castle.

## KASOS

This tiny island, almost nudging Karpathos, is 17 km long and about 4 km wide. A mountain range extends the length of the island and the south coast is almost inaccessible. On the northern side there are a number of small villages clustering around the island capital, Ophrys. Inland is a fertile plain. Access to Kasos is by inter-island steamer and also local boats from Rhodes.

Kasos has a very healthy climate. It has the following villages: **Ayia Marina, Arvanitochori, Poli, Panayia, Emboreios**.

The island has a large number of caves, of which the most interesting are those called: **tou Koraka, tis Fokokamaras, tis Plakarous, tou Moursela**. Also worth seeing are the **monastery of St. Mamas**, the **Ellinokamara** and the **ancient wall at Poli**.

## ASTYPALAEA

This Dodecanese island lies nearest the Cyclades. It has quiet beaches and many interesting local customs.

Every year, on the 15th August, which is the Day of Our Lady's Assumption, a big open-air festival is held and free food is offered to all the participants in the celebrations.

Lovely sandy beaches at: **Aghios Constantinos, Pera Aeyaio**.

## 5

## CASTELLORIZO

Castellorizo was known as Megisti in ancient times. Its first inhabitants were Achaeans. When the Turks occupied the island, it had 14,000 inhabitants; today it has 300. It is the closest Greek island to Turkey. Sights: the school building, which resembles the Athens Academy, the Cathedral with its monolithic columns, the blue cave.

# 12 cyclades

*The Cyclades form a cluster of islands in the south Aegean Sea. They are Mykonos, Delos, Tinos, Syros, Andros, Naxos, Ios, Paros, Thera or Santorini, Kea, Yaros, Kythnos, Sifnos, Milos, Kimolos, Folegandros, Sikinos, Serifos, Amorgos, Anafi and several smaller islands.*

*In addition to this, many small islets are scattered the length and breadth of the Aegean. All are notable for their picturesque scenery, their clean seas and beaches, their small towns and villages, many of which are interesting architecturally, and their historical remains, which cover all periods (prehistoric, classical, Hellenistic and Roman, Byzantine, Frankish, Turkish, and modern). The Aegean islands can offer the traveller a wide variety of types of entertainment, from the noisy international and cosmopolitan centres to the idyllic atmosphere still to be found in isolated villages.*

## MYKONOS

Mykonos is one of the most characteristic of the Cycladic islands, with its white-washed houses, hundreds of churches, windmills, and stair-like narrow streets. Since the second world war, Mykonos has become a tourist centre of international fame. Foreigners find the island fascinating, with plenty to do both in the daytime and at night.

## DELOS

Not far from Mykonos lies Delos, the island of light, the rock which was once the most splendid religious, artistic and commercial centre of ancient Hellenism, mythical birthplace of the God Apollo and the Goddess Artemis. Today Delos is a vast conglomeration of ruins. Among them the most interesting are those of: the Agora, the treasuries of the various cities, the Stoa of Antigonos, the theatre, the Terrace of the Lions, the Sanctuary of the bulls, the Sanctuary of Apollo, the Dean's house and many houses with the most beautiful mosaic floors, representations of dolphins, a Satyr, and that of Dionysus with a thyrsus in one hand and a cymbal in the other astride a panther.

1. The famous Cycladic ειδώλιο of the harper, National Archaeological Museum.
2. The Venice of Mykonos, the artist' quarter.
3. The archaeological site at Delos.
4. Many of the houses which have been built in the traditional style in recent years are the work of qualified Mykonian architects and civil engineers.

2

3

*Statue from the
Terrace of the
Lions in the ruined
ancient city
of Delos.*

## TINOS

Close to Mykonos is another pretty little Cycladic island, Tinos, with characteristic buildings of popular architecture, dovecots which are truly works of art. Its chief attraction,though, is the white marble **Church of Our Lady of the Annunciation**, the Lourdes of Greece. Near the Church are a picture gallery with works by Tinian painters and an archaeological museum with finds from the ancient temple of Amphitriti and Poseidon and from chance discoveries all over the island.

## SYROS

Syros is one of the most thriving Aegean islands, both economically and culturally. Its chief town, **Hermoupolis**, capital of the Cyclades, still retains the refinements of a maritime and industrial centre. Its neoclassical buildings, such as the library, the town hall, the old "**Apollo**" **theatre** and others, are impressive for their architectural features.

Syros has also fascinating seaside and mountainous villages.

3

## ANDROS

Andros once called
Hydroussa, is the most
northerly of the Cyclades.
It has mineral springs. The
chief town of the island is
called Andros, but it is also
known as **Kato Kastro** or
**Chora**. It has many attractive
popular houses. The small
museum in the town
contains mainly ancient
incriptions from **Palaiopolis**,
built on the site of ancient
Andros. The most interesting
summer resorts are **Apikia
(or Sariza), Batsi** and
**Corthion**.

4

*1. The cove is the symbol of peace
and the ycladic dovecote of an
inimitable folk architecture.*
*2. The Church of Panaghia
Evangellistria (Our Lady of
Annunciation) of Tinos.*
*3. View of the town of Andros.*
*4. Batsi, a popular summer resort
of Andros.*
*5. Syros, view of Hermoupolis and
its harbour.*

5

## PAROS

Paros is one of the largest of the Cycladic islands. The ancient Cretans are thought to have inhabited it. In ancient times Paros was famous for its marble which, together with that of Mount Pendeli in Attica, was what sculptors of those days used to create their superb masterpieces that today embelish many of the world's museums. Paros also had a rich intellectual and artistic tradition, as the birthplace of Scopas and Agoracritus, sculptors; Nikanor and Arkesilaos, painters; and of the celebrated satirical poet Archilochos.

Today Paros is well-known for its wonderful **Church of Panaghia "Ekatontapyliani"** (Holy Virgin of the Hundred Gates), or "Katapoliani". The main town of the island is **Paroikia**. South of it is the interesting ancient "**Grotto of the Nymphs**" and a little way beyond the ruins of a Temple of Asclepios.

4

## NAXOS

Naxos is the largest, most fertile of the Cyclades. It has vineyards, olive-groves and orchards and also grows vegetables. It also has emery and marble quarries. Naxos town is a small, picturesque town with a strong medieval character. Not far from the town are the ruins of a Mycenaean settlement and an impressive gate from the **Temple of Apollo**, built in the 6th century B.C. The museum of Naxos houses a rich collection of finds of Cycladic and Mycenaean times and some statues of classical times. The villages of the island are quiet and beautiful resorts.

*1. Panaghia Ekatontapyliani, the famous church of Paros.*
*2. General view of Parikia, capital of Paros.*
*3. Naousa, summer resort of Paros.*
*4. "Portara" in Naxos and part of the foundation of Apollo's temple, which was never completed.*
*5. View of the marina in Naxos.*

Santorini

## SANTORINI (Thera)

Thera, or Santorini, has attracted the world's attention in recent years because of the amazing descoveries of the archaeological excavations. At the south end of the island, near the village of **Acrotiri**, a whole prehistoric Minoan city has been dug up, complete with its squares, streets and two-storied houses. The excavations began in 1967 and are still going on. So far, archaeologists have uncovered finds that attest to a great civilization that was destroyed by a volcanic eruption. What really stands out from among these wonderful discoveries are the unique frescoes. They depict Springtime, Antelopes, Apes, Ladies, a fisherman, and many others, all of which have been painstakingly removed from Santorini and set in the National Archaeological Museum in Athens. Apart from the ruins, one can also visit **Phira**, the pretty township of Thera, with its white washed houses and panoramic views from the terraces. **Palaia Kameni**, the tiny isle which surfaced in the middle of the bay in 1573 A.D., still has a smouldering volcano in its centre.

## ANAFI

**Anafi** is the last of the Southwest Cyclades. It has only 400 inhabitants and nearly as many churches. There is also a castle, and a monastery built on the site of a temple of Apollo.

*1. "The Boxers", famous fresco from the archaeological site of Acrotiri, in Thera.*
*2. Representation of the volcano of Thera.*
*3. Panoramic view of Oia.*

## AMORGOS

**Amorgos**, which lies to the south-east of Naxos, is one of the prettiest islands in the Aegean. It has a population of 2,000, and is notable for its very marked Cycladic architecture. There are lots of things to see a Venetian castle, for instance, and the famous **Convent of the Presentation of the Virgin, or Chozoviotissa,** dating from Byzantine times. It contains a miraculous icon. Landings are made at **Katapola**, and the island's capital lies on a hill above, accessible by track. The remains of ancient Minoa may be seen near Katapola. **Aigiali**, second port of the island, has an acropolis which protected the ancient harbour, and the remains of a temple of Athena built into a church.

There are also a number of small islands which lie between Naxos, Ios and Amorgos. **Donousa** has four settlements, and significant remains from the geometric period in the Cyclades have been found there. **Koufonisia** (consisting of Pano Koufonisi and Kato Koufonisi) have ancient and Byzantine remains, while **Herakleia** was actually quite well known in ancient times. There is also a cave with rather impressive stalactites, and Herakleia is one of the larger of these islands. **Schoinousa** has 200 inhabitants and a few ancient ruins to show. **Karos**, however, is inhabited only by sheep and heir shepherds.

*1. Amorgos, Chozoviotissa Monastery.*
*2. A beach at Koufonissia.*
*3. Sifnos, Chrysopigi Monastery.*

1

2

3

Also in the Western Cyclades are the islands of **Kea, Kythnos, Serifos** and **Sifnos**. Sifnos is notable for its blindingly white houses and streets, and also for the extent to which local pottery has developed as a craft. At Apollonia, Vathy, Exambela, Katavatis, and Chrysopigi Byzantine churches and monasteries, ancient walls and medieval ruins may be seen.

*1. Panoramic view of Amorgos with its white traditional houses.*
*2. Kea, the nearest to Athens island of Cyclades.*
*3. A view of infertile but beautiful Kythnos.*
*4. A view of the picturesque Chora, the capital of Serifos.*

## IOS

Ios is a small island lying between Pares and Santorini (Thera). It has some small hotels, private rooms in houses and tavernas specialising in "kakavia" a kind of Greek bouillabaisse. Ios has some marvelous beaches and offers a quiet and interesting stay. It has also remains of ancient times and some 400 small chapels. In the village of **Plakoto** the inhabitants display an ancient tomb which they claim to be the tomb of Homer.

## Milos

Milos is the isle of Aphrodite and the unique catacombs. Along with Kimolos, Antimilos and Folegandros, Milos forms the western edge of the Cyclades. This is the place in which the famous statue of Aphrodite was discovered during the last century and spirited off to the Louvre in Paris, where it still remains. Near the village of **Klima** are the most important Christian catacombs in the world after those in Rome. They were built in the 1st century A.D., are 200 m. long, and their labyrinthine galleries contain 294 graves in the walls and floor, all decorated with symbols and frescoes.

1. The traditional temple of Agia Sofia, in Milos.
2. View of the island of Ios.
3. The famous statue of Aphrodite of Milos.
Opposite: The impressive rocks at Kleftiko, Milos.

# 13 crete

Crete, the largest of the Greek islands, offers yet another acceptable impression of life enhancing friendliness, beauty, fertility and the accumulated spoils of time. An island of larger space and population (500,000 inhabitants), Crete has almost unimited advantages for a holiday. The obvious ones are well known by now, but less common is the knowledge that it is fast developing into a splendidly planned holiday Island, providing excellent accomodation in first class hotels, holiday villages and garden-enclosed beach bungalow resorts designed to suit their picturesque settings. Soft sandy beaches and seas as gentle and vividly blue-to-green as any in the Mediterranean are a special delight for carefree relaxation in the sun. Yet for all the progress Crete has made in recent years, it still remains a rugged and unspoiled island.

The Cretans still live a simple life in the wild mountainous regions, or downland where vineyards and vast orchards of oranges and citrus fruit slope gently to villages and townships. An east to west road roughly follows the northern coast with well-surfaced access roads branching off at various points to lead to towns and places of historical and sightsseing interest. Remains of every period of Crete's history lie scattered everywhere, dating from the early Cretan and Minoan cultures to the more recent shelled buildings of the epic Battle of Crete in May 1941.

One can get to Crete either by air from Athens or by ship from Piraeus. The superb Minoan civilisation, destroyed sometime in 1400 B.C., was developed in Crete. The many ruins of that civilisation which exist on the island have stirred world interest for many years. In comparison with that ancient civilization and the heights it reached we can say that the later Classical and Roman ages were periods of decline for Crete.

In 824 A.D. it was captured by the Arabs who turned it into a Saracen Pirates's lair from where they launched their raids in the Mediterranean regions.

They were driven away by the Byzantine General Nicephoros Phocas (who later became Emperor of the Byzantine Empire). About 250 years later the Venetians came to Crete. Under their rule the island knew economic and intellectual development, but this was curtailed when the Turks occupied the island in 1699. For as long as the Turkish yoke lasted the Cretans never ceased fighting for their freedom which they finally regained in 1912, when the island became part of the Greek nation.

A mountainous, elongated island, averaging about 55 km in width and stretching for some 264 km from east to west, Crete is as diverse in character as the rest of Greece.

A chain of high mountains (Dikti 2,142 m., Idi 2,456 m. and the White Mountains or Lefka Ori 2,454 m.), divide it into four distinct regions whose alteranting scenery combines to form the impressive beauty of the Cretan landscape. These high mountain ranges, with their natural divisions, form the island's four provinces: Chania, Rethymnon, Heraklion and Lassithi.

## 3  HERAKLION

Heraklion, the medieval Candia, is Crete's main port of entry for visitors arriving by sea or air. This flourishing town is doubtless of some importance since it is in its vicinities that the splendid finds and art treasures of the Cretan cultures have been found.

Meraklion itself was once a Venetian leading port in the Eastern Mediterranean and remains of the 16th century wall they built round the city are still well preserved. Other interesting sights include Morosini's Fountain, St Mark's Church, the Venetian Fortress, the Loggia, St Minas Church and the bazaar.

Heraklion is the capital and administrative center of Crete, with 150,000 inhabitants.

*1. The Phaestos Disk.*
*2. The snake goddess from Knossos (1600 BC).*
*3. The kule that protects the Venetian harbor.*

*Below: The harbor of Chersonissos, with organized tourist facilities and abundant nightlife.*

The Archaeological Museum contains the richest collection of objects dating from all era of the Minoan Civilization. Its twenty halls are filled with masterpieces from Knossos, Phaestos, Malia, Aghia Triada and other archaeological sites in Crete.

## KNOSSOS

Crete's greatest attraction is indisputably Knossos, just 5 km outside Heraklion. The most interesting ruins are the reconstructed palace and the regions round it, including the Propulaea, the long passageways, the storehouses, porches and courtyards. The Palace of Minos included the magnificent pillared flight of stairs the maize of rooms, and the throne-room of the oldest of the great kingdoms of Europe.

The graceful, high-backed throne, carved in stone is still in position where it had been flanked by frescoes of griffins. But to the modern mind the great marvel in Knossos is the elaborate sanitary system of the palace.

The labyrinth of rooms was grouped about a central court, with walls glowing with brightly coloured frescoes and tiled floors, and equipped with well designed systems of ventilation, lighting and drainage. Beyond the palace walls were the dwellings of the people. They were built of stone, brick or wood, with plastered walls and flagstoned floors. Many were two or more storeys and has six or eight rooms.

The frescoes on the palace walls show people on holiday, sitting in ranks in a stadium, the women gossiping and chattering. A bull-game, shown in a palace fresco, depicts a young acrobat grasping the horns of a charging bull and hurling in a somersault over its back to be caught in the arms of a girl acrobat as he lands

The Minoan women seemed to favour large and shady hats trimmed with ribbon, and very low-necked dresses with puffed out sleeves, wasp waists and flounced skirts. Their bosoms were bare or very lightly veiled, which prompted a Frenchman to exclaim when he saw the Cretan statuettes for the first time: "These are Parisiennes!".

Knossos is vastly intricate. A maze-like structure, the Labyrinth of tradition. The word derives from "Labrys" the Lydian term for double-axe. This emblem was the symbol of the palace of Knossos, since it occurs so many times on the masonry and as a motif of decoration.

*1. Rhyton in the shape of a bull's head, from the Place of Zakros (1700-1400 BC, Archaeological Museum of Heraklion).*
*2. The fresco with the Griffins, decorating the Throne Room in Knossos.*

## Phaestos, Gortyna, Aghia Triada

Another Minoan palace has been found in the ruins of **Phaestos** (64 km from Heraklion). It has an imposing entrance with remarkable enormous flight of steps.

Phaestos was a rival city of **Gortyna** (47 km from Heraklion) where were found many interesting inscriptions and among them the famous "Code of Gortyna" (a stone plaque with the laws of the city of the 6th century B.C.).

The ruins of a Minoan villa have been found at **Aghia Triada** (13 km from Phaestos, close to the sea), as well as some beautiful Cretan vases and gobbets.

Eastwards from Heraklion, along a good asphalt road which follows the contours of the coast in a series of serpentine bends, there are empty beaches, bays and plains that slope down to the sea. Where the land is already townscape there are hotels, bungalows and restaurants.

## Mallia

The remairs of this Minoan Palace are similar to those of Knossos and Phaestos. Walk around and photograph this enigmatic palace, and then make your way down to the fabulous beach.

*3. The reconstructed west Bastion in the Palace of Knossos.*

3

## CHANIA

The old town, next to the sea, with its tall handsome houses and narrow streets, retains much of its Venetian character. At its centre rises the "**Kasteli**", a Venetian fortress. The new town is pleasant and lively, with large and modern houses which stand in gardens filled with flowers all the year round. In its outlying districts there are countless orange groves which fill the air with their aroma during orange blossom time. Several roads lead from Chania to the various beaches in the vicinity and to inland regions, as far as the shores of the Lybian Sea.

Chania is Crete's capital and administrative centre, with some 50,000 inhabitants. It has little archaeological interest but holds the tomb and house of Eleftherios Venizelos, the great statesman and Crete's most illustrius son. Also of interest in Chania is the vast naval harbour of **Suda Bay**. Above Suda are the remains of ancient **Aptera**. Crete's southern shores are rugged with high cliffs rising sheer and grim from the sea. In between there are several long stretches of beach and fishing villages full of solitude and isolated splendour.

*1. The Gates are the most imposing part of the Gorge. After we pass through them, we can see the Lybyan Sea in the distance.*
*2. View of the harbor of Chania.*
*3. Elafonisi.*

## RETHYMNON

Rethymnon lies 78 km west of Heraklion. It is a charming small town, with a history that goes back to the 4th century B.C. It flourished mainly under Venetian rule, when it made a fantastic headway as the arts and learning are concerned.

The Venetian touch is still prominent in many parts of the town, best seen in the narrowness of the streets, the old mansions and its fortress, known locally as the **Fortetza**. Two interesting sights nearby are the **Monastery of Arcadi** and the **Preveli Monastery**. In the background behind the town towers the snow-capped Mount Psiloritis or Idi. The town itself looks on to the sea and two harbours, one small and pretty, the other big and bustling with activity. It is still a pleasure to walk along the narrow, white streets of Rethymnon gazing at the marvellous mixture of architectures. More important, there are several good hotels in and out of town, beaches, flowers and woods, set against an enticing mountain background. The historical Arcadi Monastery is only 23 km away along a scenic route. The monastery has been restored since 1866, when it was burned down along with some 1,000 men, women and children who had sought refuge in it from the Turks. It is now a venerated symbol of Cretan independence and the holocaust is celebrated each year on November 8th.

*1. General view of the town of Rethymnon.*
*2. The estuaries of Kourtaliotis, the river that runs through the Kourtaliotiko Gorge.*
*3. The church of Arcadi Monastery.*

## Lassithi

**Lassithi Plateau**, with its 10,000 windmills leisurely cnurning the air, lies off the main road to Malia. The road zig-zags up the mountain until suddenly the whole plain spreads out below, fertile and cultivated.

## AGHIOS NIKOLAOS

From Malia a smooth and easy drive will take you to Crete's tourist show place — the lovely **Gulf of Mirabello**. The two great concentrations of hotels and bungalow resorts are at **Elounda** and **Aghios Nikolaos** with its cluster of white houses linked with the colourful fishing port by narrow streets.

## Sitia

Sitia stands at the other end of the gulf. It is a pleasant town and port dominated by its Venetian fort. Life centres round the waterfront and you can have a good meal at one of the local tavernas before setting out for **Kato Zakro**, the smallest and most recently excavated Minoan Palace. **Vai** on the easternmost tip of Crete is Europe's only palm tree forest. There are some 5.000 palm trees sloping down to a lake like blue sea.

## Ierapetra

Ierapetra is the only town on the southern coast of Crete. It is a prosperous agricultural centre with long stretches of beach on either side. The people live off fishing, vegetable growing and tourism. The town's strong oriental flavour comes from its maze of alleyways lined with single storey houses which must have been owned by Muslims once. There are flowers and greenery on balconies, windows, courtyards and gardens. The town's other attractions are its Venetian fortress and 18th century mosque. The waterfront is lined with tavernas. For a luxurious dip in the sea go to the east of the town, or hire a boat and head for the coves and rocks nearby. An interesting excursion is to the banana plantations and orange grove of **Mirtos**.

1. Elounda, the most cosmopolitan resort of Crete.
2. The islet-castle of Spinalonga.
3. Night view of Agios Nikolaos.
4. The beach of Siteia, in the end of Mirabello Gulf.
5. Panoramic view of Ierapetra, to the south of Crete.

Texts: MARY MC CALLUM
Artistic Supervision: PANAGIOTIS SMYRNIS
Photographs: Archive MICHALIS TOUBIS S.A.

Production - Printing: EDITIONS MICHALIS TOUBIS